Layout: **ASSIMIL** France

© Assimil 2011   ISBN 978-2-7005-0431-6
ISSN 2109-6643

This book is adapted from the German original **Russisch, Wort Für Wort** by Reise Know-How Verlag Peter Rump GmbH, Bielefeld. Copyright Peter Rump

Russian phrasebook

Elke Becker
English adaptation by Madeleine Grieve

Illustrations by J.-L. Goussé

B.P. 25
94431 Chennevières sur Marne Cedex
FRANCE

Assimil
on the Road

Languages available in this series:

- **Dutch**
- **French**
- **German**
- **Italian**
- **Russian**
- **Spanish**

Assimil on the Road, An Original Recipe

Our Ingredients:

- a splash of condensed grammar
- a good dose of conversation, based on a healthy variety of subjects
- a sprinkle of friendly advice and insider info on local customs
- to spice up the menu, a hint of humor with illustrations to make you laugh
- and to top the cake, six brilliant panel flaps to whet your appetite

All you have to do now is to pull up to the table and dig in to this balanced meal. Savor your newfound confidence and enjoy communicating with locals.

An Assimil "On the Road" phrase book is not intended to replace a language course, but if you invest a little time reading it and learning a few key phrases, you'll soon be able to communicate in another language. That will change your whole experience of traveling because you'll be more than just an ordinary tourist!

A Word of Friendly Advice: don't try to be perfect! The native speakers you talk with will forgive you the little mistakes you'll probably make at first. **The main thing is to let go of your fear and start speaking.**

CONTENTS

INTRODUCTION

Russia and the Russians 1
The Russian Language 2
The Russian Cyrillic Alphabet 3
How to Use this Book 4
   Grammar 4
   Conversation 5
   Glossary 5
   Literal Translations 5
   Abbreviations Used in this Phrase Book 8
Phonetic Transcription and Pronunciation 8
   Hard and Soft Sounds 13
   Voiced and Unvoiced Consonants 13
   Double Consonants 14
   Clusters 14
   Silent Letters 14
   Stress 14
Survival Words 15
   Is there (any)...? 16
   Do you have...? 16
   How much does... cost? 17
   Where is...? / Is there a...? 18

GRAMMAR

Common Nouns 21
   Gender 21
   The Plural 22
   Articles 23
Demonstrative Adjectives/Pronouns 24

VII

- Adjectives 24
  - Sentences with No Verb 25
  - Useful Adjectives 27
  - Colors 29
- Comparative and Superlative 29
  - More... or Less.... 29
  - The Most.... 30
  - Comparisons 32
- Adverbs 33
  - Key Adverbs 33
  - Adverbs of Time, Place, etc. 33
- Personal Pronouns 34
- Possessive Pronouns 34
- Sentence Structure 35
- Verbs 36
  - The Infinitive 36
  - The Present Tense 36
  - Aspect 38
  - The Imperfective Aspect 39
  - The Perfective Aspect 40
  - The Past Tense 41
  - The Future Tense 42
  - Modal Verbs 43
  - To Be and To Have 49
  - Verbs of Motion 52
  - Reflexive Verbs 53
  - Irregular Verbs 55
  - The Imperative 56
- Conjunctions 59
- The Six Cases 60
  - Case 1: The Nominative 60
  - Case 2: The Genitive 61
  - Case 3: The Dative 62
  - Case 4: The Accusative 62
  - Case 5: The Instrumental 63
  - Case 6: The Locative 63
- Declensions 64
  - Declension of Common Nouns 64
  - Declension of Soft-Ending Nouns 66
  - Declension of Personal Pronouns 66
- Negation 68
  - **Нет** and **Не** 68
  - Negation of **Есть** 70

Prepositions Case By Case 71
   Prepositions that Take the Genitive (Case 2)......... 71
   Prepositions that Take the Dative (Case 3) 72
   Prepositions that Take the Accusative (Case 4) 72
   Prepositions that Take the Instrumental (Case 5)..... 73
   Prepositions that Take the Locative (Case 6) 73
Questions 74
   Closed Questions............................. 74
   Open Questions.............................. 76
Numbers 79
   Cardinal Numbers 79
   Counting.................................... 81
   Ordinal Numbers 82
Age.. 83
Weights and Measures 85

CONVERSATION

Mini Guide to Russian Etiquette 87
   Sign Language 88
Time... 88
   Key Words 88
   Telling the Time 89
   Seasons 92
   Holidays.................................... 92
   Days of the Week............................. 93
   Months..................................... 94
   Dates 94
Names and Terms of Address 95
Saying Hello.................................. 97
Saying Goodbye............................... 99
Asking, Thanking, Being Polite.................. 100
   Asking for Something 100
   Saying Thank You............................ 102
   Wishing 102
   Apologizing, Expressing Regret................. 104
Accepting and Refusing 104
   Accepting and Complimenting.................. 104
   Refusing and Disagreeing..................... 105
Introductions 106
   Striking Up a Conversation.................... 107
Invitations....................................112

IX

Family	114
Love Matters...	115
Toilets	116
Insults	118
Finding Your Way Around Town	118
Directions	120
Public Transportation	122
Taxis	123
Traveling by Train	125
Traveling by Car	128
Road Signs	130
At the Service Station	131
Breakdowns	132
Road Accidents	133
Traveling by Plane or Boat	134
Traveling by Plane	134
Traveling by Boat	135
Accomodation and Meals	136
At the Hotel	136
Camping	138
At the Restaurant	139
Shopping	144
Food and Spices	147
At the Bank	148
Currencies	149
At the Post Office	150
Using the Telephone	151
Formalities	152
Filling Out a Form	152
Customs	154
Police	154
Taking Photographs	155
Smoking / No Smoking?	156
Health	157
At the Doctor's	157
At the Dentist's	159
At the Pharmacy	160

GLOSSARY

Russian – English	165
English – Russian	180

INTRODUCTION

RUSSIA AND THE RUSSIANS

If you are planning a trip to Russia, you might have already asked yourself the following questions: What is Russia like today compared with the Soviet Union? What is the population of Russia? Where is Russian spoken? Congratulations if you already know the answers, but you must admit that after the enormous political and economic changes that have taken place in Russia since the break-up of the Soviet Union, not many people know these facts off the top of their heads:

- All the former Soviet republics except the three Baltic states (Estonia, Latvia and Lithuania) joined the Commonwealth of Independent States (CIS). Turkmenistan and Georgia have since withdrawn. The CIS has a population of 200 million, of which 142 million live in the Russian Federation.
- Russian as a native language: More than 80% of the 142 million people living in the Russian Federation speak Russian as their native language. Some 30 million Russians live outside Russia, mostly in other former Soviet republics.
- Russian as a second language: the non-ethnic Russians in the Russian Federation (almost 20% of the population) represent some 100 ethnic minorities, most of which have their own languages, but they also speak Russian.

Russian was the official language in the 15 constituent republics of the Soviet Union. It was the language of education, employment, government and public life generally. Even today, most adults in the former Soviet republics understand Russian and do not mind using it (especially with tourists), even if it is not their native language. Russian is often still the language used to communicate with foreigners, including in the republics that have adopted a new official language.

The geographic distribution of countries where Russian is spoken has changed since the collapse of the Soviet Union, as independent republics have promoted other official languages and as ethnic Russians who were living in other republics have returned to Russia or emigrated, notably to Israel, where Russian speakers now make up one-fifth of the population. The Russian language nevertheless continues to be widely spoken in Ukraine and Belarus, as well as in the Baltics, the Caucasus and Central Asia. It is also one of the six official languages of the United Nations.

THE RUSSIAN LANGUAGE

Unlike English, spoken Russian is fortunately fairly close to the written language. Compared with other languages, differences between dialects are also minor. That makes it easy to understand and communicate with most Russian speakers.

Russian pronunciation can be divided into three major groups: the northern dialects, the southern dialects and the central dialects. The main difference between these groups is the way unstressed **o** is pronounced. In the northern dialects, **o** is pronounced at its full value (*aw*) whether stressed or unstressed, a pronunciation trait known as **оканиe** (*awkaniye*). In the southern and central dialects, unstressed **o** is pronounced like an **a**, a pronunciation trait known as **аканиe** (*akaniye*). The central dialects (chiefly the Moscow dialect) are considered to represent standard Russian.

As a beginner, do not worry too much about these finer points. People will understand you even if your pronunciation isn't perfect. However, we thought it was important to explain these differences to help you understand Russians from different regions.

THE RUSSIAN CYRILLIC ALPHABET

The Russian Cyrillic alphabet dates from the ninth century. It was introduced by Saints Cyril and Methodius who set out to convert the Slavic peoples to Christianity. Many letters were borrowed from the Greek and Roman alphabets, others come from Hebrew and Coptic, and some are unique to Cyrillic. The alphabet was originally used to write the language spoken by the two monks from Salonika, old Church Slavonic, which is still used today as the liturgical language in the Russian Orthodox Church. Traditionally used by six Slavic languages (Ukrainian, Belarusian, Bulgarian, Serbian, Macedonian and Russian), the Cyrillic alphabet was imposed on most of the non-Slavic republics of the Soviet Union by Stalin and adopted by Mongolia.

Today the Cyrillic alphabet is used to write Azeri, Belarusian, Bulgarian, Kazakh, Kyrgyz, Mongolian, Uzbek, Russian, Serbian, Turkmen, Tajik (although in May 2008, Tajikistan declared its intention to switch back to the Persian alphabet) and Ukrainian. Of the languages in the former USSR, only Latvian, Lithuanian, Estonian, Georgian and Armenian were never Cyrillized. With the accession of Bulgaria to the European Union on January 1, 2007, Cyrillic became the third official alphabet of the European Union.

The modern Cyrillic alphabet has 33 letters. Most of the letters are pronounced like English. The differences are explained in detail in the chapter on **Phonetic Transcription and Pronunciation**. To spell a word out loud (or recite the alphabet), here is how you say the names of the letters of the alphabet in Russian:

А, а	*ah*	Л, л	*el*	Ч, ч	*cheh*
Б, б	*beh*	М, м	*em*	Ш, ш	*sha*
В, в	*veh*	Н, н	*en*	Щ, щ	*shcha*
Г, г	*geh*	О, о	*aw*	Ъ, ъ	*tvyawrdeey znak*
Д, д	*deh*	П, п	*peh*		*(indicates a preceding hard sound)*
Е, е	*yeh*	Р, р	*air*		
Ё, ё	*yaw*	С, с	*es*	Ы, ы	*ee*
Ж, ж	*zheh*	Т, т	*teh*	Ь, ь	*myakhkiy znak*
					(indicates a preceding soft sound)
З, з	*zeh*	У, у	*oo*	Э, э	*eh*
И, и	*i*	Ф, ф	*ef*	Ю, ю	*yoo*
Й, й	*i-kratkaye*	Х, х	*kha*	Я, я	*ya*
К, к	*ka*	Ц, ц	*tseh*		

HOW TO USE THIS BOOK

This phrase book is divided into three sections:

Grammar

In this book, grammatical explanations are kept to a minimum. The basic rules are set out as simply as possible. Exceptions and irregular forms are not covered in detail. You can also skip directly to the conversation section, and just refer to the grammar section when you need information about a particular grammar point. However, the grammar section contains many useful sample sentences, not all of which appear in the **Conversation** section.

Conversation

You'll find examples and model sentences from daily life in Russia. These simple sentences will help you understand how the Russian language "works" and get you ready to converse with Russians...

For easy reference, the sentences are grouped thematically (***Saying hello***, ***Thanking***, ***Apologizing***, etc.).

Glossary

The glossary at the end of the book is divided into two parts (Russian-English and English-Russian) and altogether contains approximately 2,000 useful words. Many of the words will be new to you, since they do not appear in the ***Conversation*** section.

With help from the literal translations, you can take the examples from the conversation section and insert words from the glossary to create your own sentences. Try to see the sentences in the book as models with interchangeable components (nouns, verbs, etc.). With a little imagination, confidence and practice, you'll soon find yourself speaking Russian! The sentences you make might not all be grammatically perfect, but they'll enable you to communicate.

Literal Translations

The order of the words (subject, verb, object) in a sentence differs from one language to another. When the Russian word order differs from English, a literal English translation in smaller type is provided underneath the Russian sentence (in bold) and the phonetic transcription (in italics, see below). The literal translation is a word-for-word translation of the sentence, which follows the Russian word order (even if it doesn't make sense in English). If it takes more than one English word to translate a Russian word, these words are linked by hyphens. The bottom line in each set is a "natural" English translation.

Можно пройти пешком.
ma<u>w</u>zhna pray<u>ti</u> pishk<u>aw</u>m
it-is-possible to-go on-foot
We can walk there.

• A slash between two words means you can choose which word you want to use:

Я англичанка/американка/австралийка.
ya anglich<u>a</u>nka/amyirik<u>a</u>nka/afstral<u>i</u>yka
I English-woman/American-woman/Australian-woman
I am English/American/Australian.

• A slash is also used to separate the masculine and feminine forms:

Я рад/рада.
ya rat/r<u>a</u>da
I glad-[m./f.]
I'm glad.

Я писал/писала письмо.
ya pis<u>a</u>l/pis<u>a</u>la pis^ym<u>aw</u>
I wrote-[m./f.] letter
I wrote a letter.

Ты согласен/согласна?
tee sagl<u>a</u>syin/sagl<u>a</u>sna
you-[informal] in-agreement-[m./f.]
Do you agree?

Вы согласны?
vwee sagl<u>a</u>snee
you-[formal/plural] in-agreement-[pl.]
Do you agree?

In the first three sentences above, use the first form of the word if the subject is a man and the second form if the subject is a woman. The second sentence shows another feature of Russian: in the past tense, verb endings change with the gender of the subject.

In the last two sentences, you can see that there are two words meaning *you* in Russian. **Ты** is the informal singular *you*, which you use to address a person you know well, a child or a pet. The adjective is singular and masculine or feminine depending on whether *you* is male or female. **Вы** can be either the formal singular *you*, when you are speaking to an adult you do not know well, or the plural *you*, when you are speaking to more than one person, regardless of how well you know them. Whether **вы** is singular or plural, the adjective that goes with it is always plural.

• When the verb ending does not indicate the gender or when the pronoun is left out in Russian, we indicate the gender and/or person in square brackets in the literal translation:

Пойдёмте купаться!
paydyawmtye koopat'sa
[we]-go to-bathe-self
Let's go swimming!

• In Russian, noun, adjective and pronoun endings change according to the function of the word in the sentence (subject, direct object, indirect object, etc.). These changes are known as "cases". There are six cases in Russian. In the literal translation, a number from 2 to 6 is shown in superscript after the word to indicate case:

С удовольствием!
s-oodavawl'ʲstviyim
with pleasure[5]
With pleasure!

Abbreviations Used in this Phrase Book

m.	masculine	2	genitive
f.	feminine	3	dative
n.	neuter	4	accusative
sg.	singular	5	instrumental
pl.	plural	6	locative
=	singular and plural are the same	uni.	unidirectional
!	imperative	multi.	multidirectional
perf.	perfective verb	adv.	adverb
II	verb with stem in **o** *aw*	adj.	adjective
III	verb with stem in **и** *i*	impers.	impersonal
		irreg.	irregular

PHONETIC TRANSCRIPTION AND PRONUNCIATION

To help you decipher all the Russian words and texts in this pocket guidebook, a phonetic transcription is used. The Cyrillic word is followed by a transcription in Roman letters that is as close as possible to the Russian pronunciation. This system will enable you to read, understand and learn new words easily. As far as possible, we avoid using unfamiliar letters or signs, but in some rare cases when it is not possible to do otherwise, we explain how these are pronounced. The stressed vowels in each word are underlined. The table below contains a complete list of the phonetic transcription of all the letters in the Russian alphabet (in upper and lower case) and their pronunciation, which changes for some letters depending on their position in the word.

Cyrillic	Transc.	Sounds like	Examples
А, а	a	as in **h**a**r**d	ма́ма m**a**ma mom
	i	as in **i**t (unstressed before stressed syllable)	часы́ ch**i**see watch
Б, б	b	as in **b**at	ба́бочка b**a**bachka butterfly
	p	as in **p**ot (when before an unvoiced consonant or when final letter)	ю́бка y**oo**pka skirt
В, в	v	as in **v**at	во́дка v**a**wtka vodka
	f	as in **f**at (when before an unvoiced consonant or when final letter)	о́стров **a**wstraf island
Г, г	g	as in **g**et	гру́ша gr**oo**sha pear
	k	as in **k**ick	друг dr**oo**k friend
Д, д	d	as in **d**og	дом d**a**wm house
	t	as in **t**op	мёд my**a**wt honey
Е, е	ye	as in **ye**s (stressed or when final letter)	де́вушка d**ye**vooshka young woman
	yi	as in **yi**n (unstressed)	сестра́ s**yi**stra sister
	e	as in **e**nd (after ж, ц and ш)	же́нщина zh**e**nshchina woman
Ё, ё	yaw	as in **yaw**n	ёлка **yaw**lka fir tree, Christmas tree

де́вять

	aw	as in *dawn* (after ж, ц and ш)	мёлтый *zhawlteey* yellow
Ж, ж	zh	as in *treasure*	жена *zheena* wife
	sh	as in *shop*	этаж *itash* storey
З, з	z	as in *zoo*	зал *zal* room
	s	as in *sit*	газ *gas* gas
И, и	i	as in *it*	привет *privyet* hi
	ee	as in *peek* (after ж, ц and ш)	жить *zheet^s* to live
Й, й	y	as in *boy*	мой *moy* my, mine
К, к	k	as in *kick*	кот *kawt* cat
	g	as in *get* (before a voiced consonant)	вокзал *vagzal* railway station
Л, л	l	as in *let*	лес *lyes* forest
М, м	m	as in *met*	мост *mawst* bridge
Н, н	n	as in *net*	нос *naws* nose
О, о	aw	as in *thaw* (stressed)	сок *sawk* juice
	a	as in *hard* (unstressed)	хорошо *kharashaw* good, well
	o	as in *boy* (when followed by й and stressed)	большой *bal^yshoy* big
П, п	p	as in *pot*	парк *park* park
Р, р	r	rolled r as in Scots *rock* or Italian *arrivederci*	спорт *spawrt* sport
С, с	s	as in *sit*	сумка *soomka* bag
	z	as in *zoo* (before a voiced consonant)	сдача *zdacha* change
Т, т	t	as in *top*	тариф *tarif* tariff

У, у	oo	as in l*oo*k	**университет** oo*nivyirsit*y*et* university
Ф, ф	f	as in *f*at	**фрукт** *f*rookt fruit
Х, х	kh	as in Scots lo*ch* or German Ba*ch*	**выход** v*wee*khat exit
Ц, ц	ts	as in lo*ts*	**гостиница** gas*ti*nitsa hotel
Ч, ч	ch	as in *ch*ore	**почта** p*aw*chta post office, mail
	sh	as in hu*sh* (before н and in что)	**конечно** kany*e*shna of course **что** shtaw what, that
Ш, ш	sh	as in hu*sh*	**школа** shk*aw*la school
Щ, щ	shch	as in fre*sh ch*eese	**овощи** <u>aw</u>vashchi vegetables
Ъ, ъ	°	the hard sign hardens a preceding consonant that would otherwise be soft because followed by a soft vowel	**отъезжать** at°yezhzha*t*ˢ to leave (in a vehicle)
Ы, ы	ee	as in p*ee*k but pronounced with the tongue back as far back as possible. Try merging an *oo* and an *ee* sound.	**ты** t*ee* you
	wee	as in bet*wee*n (after б, в and м)	**мы** m*wee* we
Ь, ь	ʸⁱ	the soft sign is not pronounced by itself, but it softens	**здесь** zdyesʸⁱ here

одиннадцать 11

		(or "palatalizes") the preceding consonant by adding a very short *yi* sound after the consonant, as in **yi**n	
	s	after д and т, the soft sign is like a short *s*	**читать** *chitat^s* to read
	'	after ч, ш and щ and before some soft vowels, the soft sign is silent	**читаешь** *chitayish'* you are reading
Э, э	*e*	as in **e**nd	**этот** *etat* this
	i	as in **i**t (unstressed)	**этаж** *itash* storey
Ю, ю	*yoo*	as in d**u**ke	**слушаю** *slooshayoo* I'm listening
Я, я	*ya*	as in **ya**hoo (stressed)	**яма** *yama* hole
	yi	as in **yi**n (unstressed)	**язык** *yizeek* language, tongue

- We have endeavored to keep the phonetic transcription as close as possible to the Cyrillic spelling of the Russian words while keeping it simple in English. The transcription will enable you to read all the Russian phrases in this book straight away, without having to look up the pronunciation of each letter.
- When two words are pronounced like one word, they are joined by a hyphen in the transcription: e.g. **в город** *v-gawrat*, *into town*.

• If you have time, practice visualizing the word in Cyrillic and reading the phonetic transcription out loud. You'll soon get used to it. Even words that seem complicated at first will soon become easy to pronounce.

Hard and Soft Sounds

The difference between "hard" and "soft" vowels is important, especially when words are declined (when word endings change according to their function in the sentence).

- Hard: **а** *a*, **э** *e*, **о** *aw*, **у** *oo*, **ы** *ee*
- Soft: **я** *ya*, **е** *ye*, **ё** *yaw*, **ю** *yoo*, **и** *i*

All consonants are hard by default, but are softened if they are followed by one of the soft vowels or the soft sign **ь**. Conversely, the consonants **ж** *zh*, **ц** *ts*, **ш** *sh* harden any soft vowel that comes after them.

Voiced and Unvoiced Consonants

In Russian, as in English, there are two types of consonants: "voiced" and "unvoiced". Voiced consonants make the vocal chords vibrate and you can sing them on different notes. Unvoiced consonants do not make the vocal chords vibrate and you cannot sing them. Some consonants are always voiced – **л** *l*, **м** *m*, **н** *n*, and **р** *r*.

As the table above shows, the consonants – **б** *b*, **в** *v*, **г** *g*, **д** *d*, **ж** *zh*, and **з** *z* – are usually voiced, but become unvoiced at the end of a word or before an unvoiced consonant: **б** *p*, **в** *f*, **г** *k*, **д** *t*, **ж** *sh*, and **з** *s*.

Other consonants are usually unvoiced – **к** *k*, **с** *s* – but become voiced before a voiced consonant: **к** *g* and **с** *z*.

Double Consonants

Double consonants in Russian words are usually pronounced the same as a single consonant, unless the speaker specifically emphasizes the double consonant. Therefore the phonetic transcription only indicates a single consonant, except in cases where the consonant sounds double, especially **нн** *nn*.

Clusters

The pronunciation of some consonants also changes in some clusters.

его	*yiv<u>aw</u>*	его	*yiv<u>aw</u>*	him/his
		сегодня	*syiv<u>aw</u>dya*	today
ого	*av<u>aw</u>*	до того	*da-tav<u>aw</u>*	until then
зж	*zhzh*	приезжать	*priyizhzh<u>at</u>ᵉ*	to arrive
сч	*shch*	счастья	*shch<u>a</u>stya*	happiness
тся, ться	*tsa*	заниматься	*zanim<u>a</u>tsa*	to occupy oneself with

Silent Letters

Sometimes one or more letters in a word are silent. Examples of these exceptions are:
– the first **в** in **здравствуйте** *zdr<u>a</u>stvooytye, hello*
– the **уй** in **пожалуйста** *pazh<u>a</u>lsta, please*
– the **д** in **праздник** *pr<u>a</u>znik, holiday*
– the second **и** in **официант** *afits<u>a</u>nt, waiter*

Stress

The underlined letters indicate the syllable on which the stress falls, i.e. the syllable that is emphasized in pronunciation. The stressed vowel in a word must be pronounced clearly, at full value. Take twice as long to pronounce the stressed vowel as for the other vowels in the word. The unstressed vowels are reduced, i.e. they are shorter and less clearly articulated. This also occurs in English. In the word *intonation*, for example, the a is stressed, while unstressed vowels, particularly the preceding o, are reduced.

The stress can move in a word as it changes case.

| врач | *vrach* | doctor |
| врача | *vracha* | the doctor's (genitive case) |

In Russian, two words spelled the same way but with a different stress can have different meanings. The same thing happens in English, e.g. object/object, record/record, content/content.

| мука | *mooka* | flour |
| мука | *mooka* | torment |

SURVIVAL WORDS

да	*da*	yes
нет	*nyet*	no
спасибо	*spasiba*	thank you
пожалуйста	*pazhalsta*	please / you're welcome
Добрый день!	*dawbreey dyen*^{yi}	Hello! (good day)
До свидания!	*da svidaniya*	Goodbye!

It is polite to begin a question with one of the following constructions:

Извините, пожалуйста... / Простите, пожалуйста...	Excuse me, ...
izvinitye pazhalsta / prastitye pazhalsta	
Скажите, пожалуйста...	Can you please tell me... ?
skazheetye pazhalsta	

Покажите, пожалуйста...	Can you please show me... ?
pakazh<u>ee</u>tye pazh<u>a</u>lsta	
Дайте, пожалуйста...	Can you please give me... ?
d<u>ay</u>tye pazh<u>a</u>lsta	

The simple structure of the following sentences enables you to make your own sentences, using words from the tables (or the glossary at the back of the book).

Is there (any)...?

Есть свободная комната?	Есть пиво?
yest^s svab<u>aw</u>dnaya <u>kaw</u>mnata	yest^s p<u>i</u>va
there-is free room	there-is beer
Is there a free room?	Is there any beer?

кофе	k<u>aw</u>fye	coffee
врач	vrach	doctor
рынок	r<u>ee</u>nak	market
чай	chay	tea

Two possible answers to those questions are:

Да, есть.	Нет, этого нет.
da yest^s	nyet <u>e</u>tava nyet
yes there-is	no of-that no
Yes, there is.	No, there isn't.

Do you have...?

У вас есть билеты?
oo vas yest^s bil<u>ye</u>tee
in-the-possession of-you-[formal/plural] there-are tickets
Do you have tickets?

У вас есть карта Москвы?
oo vas yest^s k<u>a</u>rta maskvw<u>ee</u>
in-the-possession of-you-[formal/plural] there-is map of-Moscow
Do you have a map of Moscow?

Possible answers:

Affirmative:

Да, у нас есть билеты / карта Москвы.
da oo nas yest^s bil<u>ye</u>tee / k<u>a</u>rta maskvw<u>ee</u>
yes in-the-possession of-us there-is/are tickets / map of-Moscow
Yes, we have tickets / a map of Moscow.

Да, есть.
da yest^s
yes there-is
Yes, we do.

Negative:

Нет, у нас нет билетов / карты Москвы.
nyet oo nas nyet bily<u>e</u>taf / k<u>a</u>rtee maskvw<u>ee</u>
no in-the-possession of-us no of-tickets / of-map of-Moscow
No, we don't have tickets / a map of Moscow.

Нет, нету.
nyet ny<u>e</u>too
no no
No, we don't.

How much does... cost?

Сколько стоит комната/билет?
sk<u>awl</u>^yka st<u>aw</u>it k<u>aw</u>mnata/bil<u>ye</u>t
how-much costs room/ticket
How much does a room/ticket cost?

Сколько это стоит?
sk<u>awl</u>^yka <u>e</u>ta st<u>aw</u>it
how-much this costs
How much does this cost?

У ВАС ЕСТЬ КАРТА МОСКВЫ?
(Do you have a map of Moscow?)

Answer:

>Это стоит...
>*eta stawit*
>that costs
>It costs...

Numbers are explained in the chapter on numbers.

Where is...? / Is there a...?

Где гостиница?
gdye gastinitsa
where hotel
Where is there a hotel?

Где такси?
gdye taksi
where taxi
Where can we find a taxi?

Где находится музей?
gdye nakhawditsa moozyey
where finds-self museum
Where is the museum? /
Where is there a museum?

Где находится больница?
gdye nakhawditsa bal'nitsa
where finds-self hospital
Where is the hospital?

аэропорт	_airapawrt_	airport
банк	_bank_	bank
консульство	_kawnsool^{yi}stva_	consulate
посольство	_pasawl^{yi}stva_	embassy
аптека	_aptyeka_	pharmacy
милиция	_militseeya_	police
почта	_pawchta_	post office
вокзал	_vagzal_	railway station
ресторан	_ryistaran_	restaurant
телефон	_tyilyifawn_	telephone
туалет	_tooalyet_	toilet
мастерская	_mastyirskaya_	workshop
здесь	_zdyes^{yi}_	here
там	_tam_	there / over there
справа	_sprava_	right
слева	_slyeva_	left
направо	_naprava_	on the right
налево	_nalyeva_	on the left
прямо	_pryama_	straight ahead
назад	_nazat_	back
далеко	_dalyikaw_	far
недалеко	_nyidalyikaw_	near
перекрёсток	_pyiryikryawstak_	intersection, crossroads
светофор	_svyitafawr_	traffic light
за городом	_za-garadam_	outside the city
в центре	_f-tsentrye_	in the city center

GRAMMAR

COMMON NOUNS

Gender

Unlike in English, all Russian nouns have a grammatical gender, not just animate nouns that have a natural gender as in English (e.g. boy is masculine). There are three grammatical genders in Russian: masculine (m.), feminine (f.) and neuter (n.). In the three groups, a distinction is made between soft-ending and hard-ending nouns. It is usually possible to tell the gender of a noun from its ending.

masculine		
hard	any consonant	**театр** *tyiatr* theater
soft	**-й** *y*	**трамвай** *tramvay* tram
	-ь *yi/s*	**рубль** *roobl^{yi}* ruble
feminine		
hard	**-а** *a*	**комната** *k<u>aw</u>mnata* room
soft	**-я** *ya / yi*	**неделя** *nyid<u>ye</u>lya* week
	-ь *yi/s*	**тетрадь** *tyitr<u>at</u>^{s}* exercise book
neuter		
hard	**-о** *aw / a*	**место** *m<u>ye</u>sta* place
soft	**-е** *ye*	**море** *m<u>aw</u>rye* sea

The grammatical gender of animate nouns is the same as their natural gender (e.g. boy is masculine).

двадцать один 21

папа (m.)	*papa*	dad
мать (f.)	*mat*^{s}	mother
сын (m.)	*seen*	son

стюардесса (f.)	*styooardyesa*	stewardess
официант (m.)	*afitsant*	waiter
девушка (f.)	*dyevooshka*	young woman

When the gender of a word is not obvious, it is indicated between brackets after the word: (m.) for masculine, (f.) for feminine, (n.) for neuter.

The Plural

The use of the plural after numbers is unusual in Russian (see ***Counting***).

The plural ending of hard-ending masculine and feminine nouns is **-ы** *ee*. The plural ending of soft-ending masculine and feminine nouns is **-и** *i/ee*.
To form the plural of hard-ending masculine nouns, **-ы** *ee* is simply added to the end of the singular form. To form the plural of other masculine and feminine nouns, **-ы** *ee* or **-и** *i/ee* replaces the last letter of the singular form.

театр (m.)	*tyiatr*	theater
театры	*tyiatree*	theaters
трамвай (m.)	*tramvay*	tram
трамваи	*tramvai*	trams
рубль (m.)	*roobl*^{yi}	ruble
рубли	*roobli*	rubles
комната (f.)	*kawmnata*	room
комнаты	*kawmnatee*	rooms
неделя (f.)	*nyidyelya*	week
недели	*nyidyeli*	weeks
тетрадь (f.)	*tyitrat*^{s}	exercise book
тетради	*tyitradi*	exercise books

The plural ending of neuter nouns is **-a** *a* for hard-ending nouns and **-я** *ya* for soft-ending nouns. The plural ending replaces the last letter of the singular form and the stress changes:

место (n.)	m*ye*sta	place
места	my*i*sta	places
море (n.)	m*aw*rye	sea
моря	mar*ya*	seas

Some masculine words are an exception to the above rule and also form their plural with **-a** *a*. The stress falls on the final letter, which is the mark of the plural:

адрес	*a*dryis	address
адреса	adryis*a*	addresses
глаз	glas	eye
глаза	glaz*a*	eyes
дом	dawm	house
дома	dam*a*	houses
город	*gaw*rat	town
города	garad*a*	towns
поезд	*paw*yist	train
поезда	payizd*a*	trains

In Russian, as in many other languages, some words are used only in the plural:

| деньги | d*yen*^{yi}gi | money (pl.) |
| каникулы | kan*i*koolee | vacation (pl.) |

Articles

Good news! Russian does not use articles, either definite (*the*) or indefinite (*a*). For example, the word **вокзал** *vagzal* can mean *the railway station* or *a railway station* or just *railway station*. Context will tell you which meaning is intended.

двадцать три

However, if you wish to say *a + noun* as in *one of something*, use the number **один** *adin*, *one*. e.g. **один литр** *adin litr*, *one liter*. See the chapter on numbers.

DEMONSTRATIVE ADJECTIVES/PRONOUNS

Demonstratives (this, that, such) always come before the noun they refer to. In the singular, they agree in gender (masculine, feminine, neuter). In the plural, they agree with the noun in number only (the plural ending does not show gender).

m.	**этот** *etat* this	**тот** *tawt* that	**такой** *takoy* such
f.	**эта** *eta* this	**та** *ta* that	**такая** *takaya* such
n.	**это** *eta* this	**то** *taw* that	**такое** *takoye* such
pl.	**эти** *eti* these	**те** *tye* those	**такие** *takiye* such

этот трамвай (m.)	*etat tramvay*	this tram
такая книга (f.)	*takaya kniga*	such a book
то кино (n.)	*taw kinaw*	that cinema
эти дети (pl.)	*eti dyeti*	these children

These demonstratives adjectives can also stand as pronouns. The neuter singular **это** *eta*, *this*, can be used to form impersonal sentences meaning "this is..." or "it's...":

Это мой друг.
eta moy drook
this my friend-[m.]
This is my (boy)friend.

Это моя подруга.
eta maya padrooga
this my friend-[f.]
This is my (girl)friend.

ADJECTIVES

As in English, Russian adjectives come before the noun they are describing. They agree with the noun in gender (masculine/feminine/neuter) and in number (singular/plural).

Most adjectives end in **-ый** *eey*. After a root that ends in a sibilant or **-г-** *g*, **-к-** *k* or **-х-** *kh*, adjectives end in **-ий** *iy* in the masculine singular. A smaller group of adjectives end in **-ой** *oy* and this syllable is always stressed.

These three basic endings (**-ый** *eey*, **-ий** *iy* and **-ой** *oy*) are the masculine singular form. The table below gives the endings for the other two genders and the plural:

Basic form = m.	красив**ый** *kras<u>i</u>vweey* beautiful	больш**ой** *bal^ysh<u>oy</u>* big	высок**ий** *vwees<u>aw</u>kiy* high
f.	красив**ая** *kras<u>i</u>vaya*	больш**ая** *bal^ysh<u>a</u>ya*	высок**ая** *vwees<u>aw</u>kaya*
n.	красив**ое** *kras<u>i</u>vaye*	больш**ое** *bal^ysh<u>a</u>wye*	высок**ое** *vwees<u>aw</u>kaye*
pl.	красив**ые** *kras<u>i</u>vweeye*	больш**ие** *bal^ysh<u>ee</u>ye*	высок**ие** *vwees<u>aw</u>kiye*

красивый человек *kras<u>i</u>vweey chyilav<u>ye</u>k*	a/the beautiful man/person
красивая девушка *kras<u>i</u>vaya dy<u>e</u>vooshka*	a/the beautiful young woman
красивое место *kras<u>i</u>vaye my<u>e</u>sta*	a/the beautiful place
красивые дети *kras<u>i</u>vweeye dy<u>e</u>ti*	beautiful children

In the glossary at the back of the book, adjectives are given in the basic form, i.e. with the masculine singular ending.

Sentences with No Verb

Now you have all the components you need to make sentences in the present tense in which the verb "to be" is understood.

In this type of sentence, the adjective appears after the noun it describes and agrees with the noun in gender and number.

Этот дом большой.
etat dawm bal[y]shoy
this house big-[m.]
This house is big.

Человек красивый.
chyilavyek krasivweey
man beautiful-[m.]
That man is handsome.

Девушка красивая.
dyevooshka krasivaya
young-woman beautiful-[f.]
That girl is beautiful.

Место красивое.
myesta krasivaye
place beautiful-[n.]
This place is beautiful.

You can also make longer sentences:

Этот новый дом большой.
etat nawwweey dawm bal[y]shoy
this new-[m.] house big-[m.]
This new house is big.

Старый человек красивый.
stareey chyilavyek krasivweey
old-[m.] man-beautiful-[m.]
That old man is handsome.

N.B. If the subject of the sentence is a personal pronoun (I, you, he, etc.), the adjective will be masculine or feminine, depending on the sex of the person concerned:

Я устал.
ya oostal
I tired-[m.]
I'm tired (man).

Я устала.
ya oostala
I tired-[f.]
I'm tired (woman).

Ты симпатичный.
tee simpatichneey
you-[informal] nice-[m.]
You're nice (of a man).

Ты симпатичная.
tee simpatichnaya
you-[informal] nice-[f.]
You're nice (of a woman).

Я устал.
(I'm tired.)

Я устала.
(I'm tired.)

From now on, the masculine and feminine forms will be separated by a slash.

The sentences on the previous page are in the present tense. To form similar sentences in the past or future tense, you need to use the verb **быть** *bweetˢ*, *to be*, in the appropriate form.

Useful Adjectives

хороший	kharawsheey	good
плохой	plakhoy	bad
большой	bal[y]shoy	big
маленький	malen[y]kiy	small
молодой	maladoy	young
старый	stareey	old
тёплый	tyawpleey	warm
холодный	khalawdneey	cold
близкий	bliskiy	near
дальний	dal[y]niy	far

красивый	*krasivweey*	beautiful
некрасивый	*nyikrasivweey*	ugly
больной	*bal^{ly}noy*	sick
здоровый	*zdarawvweey*	healthy
дорогой	*daragoy*	expensive, dear
дешёвый	*dyishawvweey*	cheap
богатый	*bagateey*	rich
бедный	*byedneey*	poor
сильный	*sil^{ly}neey*	strong
слабый	*slabweey*	weak
простой	*prastoy*	simple
сложный	*slawzhneey*	complicated
лёгкий	*lyawkhkiy*	light (weight)
тяжёлый	*tyizhawleey*	heavy
польный	*pawl^{ly}neey*	full
пустой	*poostoy*	empty
голодный	*galawdneey*	hungry
сытый	*seeteey*	full (with food)
чистый	*chisteey*	clean
грязный	*gryazneey*	dirty
длинный	*dlineey*	long
короткий	*karawtkiy*	short
высокий	*vweesawkiy*	high
низкий	*niskiy*	low
быстрый	*bweestreey*	fast
медленный	*myedlyineey*	slow
счастливый	*shchislivweey*	happy
печальный, грустный	*pyichal^{ly}neey groosneey*	sad
интересный	*intyiryesneey*	interesting
скучный	*skooshneey*	boring
умный	*oomneey*	clever
глупый	*gloopeey*	stupid
светлый	*svyetleey*	light (color)
тёмный	*tyawmneey*	dark

28   двадцать восемь

Colors

чёрный	ch**yaw**rneey	black
голубой	gal**ooboy**	blue (light ~)
синий	s**i**niy	blue (dark ~)
коричневый	kar**i**chnyivweey	brown
цветной	tsvyitn**oy**	colored
серый	s**ye**reey	gray
зелёный	zyil**yaw**neey	green
оранжевый	ar**a**nzhevweey	orange
розовый	r**aw**zavweey	pink
фиолетовый	fial**ye**tavweey	purple
красный	kr**a**sneey	red
белый	b**ye**leey	white
жёлтый	zh**aw**lteey	yellow

COMPARATIVE AND SUPERLATIVE

More... or Less...

Attributive comparative adjectives come before the noun. In English, there are two ways to form an attributive comparative adjective:
1) either a short adjective + -er (e.g. *higher*)
2) or "more" + a long adjective (e.g. *more impressive*)

The most common way to form an attributive comparative adjective in Russian is to use **более** b**aw**lyiye, *more* + long adjective. **Менее** m**ye**nyiye, *less* + long adjective is used to form a "reverse" comparative.
Более and **менее** are invariable, while the adjective agrees in gender and number with the noun it describes.

двадцать девять

менее красивый человек
myenyiye krasivweey chyilavyek
less beautiful-[m.] person
a less handsome man

более красивая девушка
bawlyiye krasivaya dyevooshka
more beautiful-[f.] young-woman
a more beautiful young woman

The Most...

Attributive superlative adjectives come before the noun. In English, there are two ways to form an attributive (coming before the noun) superlative adjective:
1) either a short adjective + -est (e.g. *highest*)
2) or "the most" + a long adjective (e.g. *the most impressive*)

In Russian, the attributive superlative of an adjective is formed using **самый** *samweey*, *the most*, before the adjective. Like the adjective, **самый** agrees in gender and number with the noun it describes.

самое красивое место
samaye krasivaye myesta
the-most-[n.] beautiful-[n.] place
the most beautiful place

самые красивые дети
samweeye krasivweeye dyeti
the-most-[pl.] beautiful-[pl.] children
the most beautiful children

To recapitulate:

сладкий	более сладкий	самый сладкий
slatkiy	*bawlyiye slatkiy*	*samweey slatkiy*
sweet (m.)	more sweet (m.)	the-most sweet (m.)
sweet	sweeter	sweetest
сладкая	более сладкая	самая сладкая
slatkaya	*bawlyiye slatkaya*	*samaya slatkaya*
sweet (f.)	more sweet (f.)	the-most sweet (f.)
sweet	sweeter	sweetest

It would be too easy if there were no exceptions to these simple rules. The six adjectives in the table below form their attributive comparatives irregularly. Except for **хороший**, the superlative forms are like other adjectives (i.e. **самый** + adjective).

хороший	лучший	самый лучший / лучший
kha<u>ra</u>wsheey	<u>loo</u>chsheey	<u>sa</u>mweey <u>loo</u>chsheey / <u>loo</u>chsheey
good	better	best
плохой	худший	самый плохой / худший
plakh<u>oy</u>	kh<u>oot</u>sheey	<u>sa</u>mweey plakh<u>oy</u> / kh<u>oot</u>sheey
bad	worse	worst
большой	больший	самый большой
bal^ysh<u>oy</u>	<u>baw</u>l^ysheey	<u>sa</u>mweey bal^ysh<u>oy</u>
big	bigger	biggest
маленький	меньший	самый маленький
<u>ma</u>lyin^ykiy	m<u>ye</u>n^ysheey	<u>sa</u>mweey <u>ma</u>lyin^ykiy
small	smaller	smallest
молодой	младший	самый молодой / самый младший
malad<u>oy</u>	ml<u>a</u>dsheey	<u>sa</u>mweey malad<u>oy</u> / <u>sa</u>mweey ml<u>a</u>dsheey
young	younger	youngest / youngest (of siblings), junior
старый	старший	самый старый / самый старший
st<u>a</u>reey	st<u>a</u>rsheey	<u>sa</u>mweey st<u>a</u>reey / <u>sa</u>mweey st<u>a</u>rsheey
old	older/elder, senior	oldest/eldest, senior

Adverbs can be formed from the comparative stems of these adjectives. Adverbs come after a verb:

лучше	<u>loo</u>chshe	better
хуже	kh<u>oo</u>zhe	worse
больше	<u>baw</u>l^yshe	bigger

меньше	*myen^yshe*	smaller
моложе	*malawzhe*	younger
старше	*starshe*	older

Comparisons

You can compare two people or two things by using **чем** *chyem*, *than*. **Чем** is preceded by a comma.

Петербург более красивый, чем Смоленск.
pyityirboork bawlyiye krasivweey chyem smalyensk
Petersburg more beautiful than Smolensk
Saint Petersburg is more beautiful than Smolensk.

Тамара более красивая, чем Мария.
tamara bawlyiye krasivaya chyem mariya
Tamara more beautiful than Maria
Tamara is more beautiful than Maria.

To compare two people or things of equal value, use **такой же..., как** *takoy zhe...kak*, *as... as...* (lit. "such-same... as"). **Такой** agrees in gender and number with the noun it describes. **Как** is preceded by a comma.

Петербург такой же красивый, как Париж.
pyityirboork takoy-zhe krasivweey kak parish
Petersburg such same beautiful as Paris
Saint Petersburg is as beautiful as Paris.

Тамара такая же красивая, как Мария.
tamara takaya-zhe krasivaya kak mariya
Tamara such same beautiful as Maria
Tamara is as beautiful as Maria.

ADVERBS

Adverbs are invariable and describe verbs, adjectives, nouns and other adverbs. They answer questions like "how?", "where?" and "when?". Most adverbs are formed on the basis of an adjective, usually by replacing the ending (**-ый** *eey*, **-ий** *iy* or **-ой** *oy*) with an **-o** *aw/a*.

хороший день
khar<u>aw</u>sheey dyen^{yi}
good-[m.] day
a good day

Он работает хорошо!
awn rab<u>aw</u>tayit kharash<u>aw</u>
he works well
He works well!

Key Adverbs

правильно	pr<u>a</u>vil^{yi}na	right
неправильно	nyipr<u>a</u>vil^{yi}na	wrong
высоко	vweesak<u>aw</u>	high/highly
глубоко	gloobak<u>aw</u>	deep/deeply
хорошо	kharash<u>aw</u>	well
плохо	pl<u>aw</u>kha	badly
быстро	bw<u>ee</u>stra	fast/quickly
медленно	m<u>ye</u>dlyinna	slowly
холодно	kh<u>aw</u>ldna	cold
тепло	tyipl<u>aw</u>	warm
весело	v<u>ye</u>syila	happily
печально	pyich<u>a</u>l^{yi}na	sadly
грязно	gr<u>ya</u>zna	dirtily
чисто	ch<u>i</u>sta	cleanly

Adverbs of Time, Place, etc.

никогда	nikagd<u>a</u>	never
всегда	fsyigd<u>a</u>	always
раньше	r<u>a</u>n^{yi}she	earlier
позже	p<u>aw</u>zhzhe	later
сегодня	syiv<u>aw</u>dnya	today

тридцать три

завтра	_za_ftra	tomorrow
вчера	f_chyi_ra	yesterday
здесь	z_dyes_ʸⁱ	here
там	_tam_	there
много	_mnaw_ga	many/much
мало	_ma_la	little/few
всё	_fsyaw_	all
ничего	ni_chyivaw_	nothing
очень	_awchyin_ʸⁱ	very
слишком	_slish_kam	too

очень хорошо
_awchyin_ʸⁱ _kharashaw_
very good

слишком большой
slishkam balʸⁱshoy
too big

PERSONAL PRONOUNS

я	_ya_	I
ты	_tee_	you (sg. informal)
он/она/оно	_awn/ana/anaw_	he/she/it
мы	_mwee_	we
вы	_vwee_	you (sg. formal/plural)
они	_ani_	they

Russian has two forms of the singular second person pronoun (you): the informal **ты** _tee_ for a close friend, a relative, a child or an animal, and the formal **вы** _vwee_ for a person you do not know well or who is your senior. **вы** is also the plural form of _you_. These distinctions are the same as French _tu_ and _vous_.

POSSESSIVE PRONOUNS

	my	your (sg. informal)	his, its	her	our	your (pl./ sg. formal)	their
m.	мой	твой	его	её	наш	ваш	их
	moy	_tvoy_	_yivaw_	_yiyaw_	_nash_	_vash_	_ikh_

34 тридцать четыре

f.	моя	твоя	его	её	наша	ваша	их
	maya	*tvaya*	*yivaw*	*yiyaw*	*nasha*	*vasha*	*ikh*
n.	моё	твоё	его	её	наше	ваше	их
	mayaw	*tvayaw*	*yivaw*	*yiyaw*	*nashe*	*vashe*	*ikh*
pl.	мои	твои	его	её	наши	ваши	их
	mayi	*tvayi*	*yivaw*	*yiyaw*	*nashee*	*vashee*	*ikh*

Unlike in English, personal pronouns agree in number and gender (feminine, masculine or neuter) in the singular and in number only in the plural with the object or person "possessed". In the third person singular and plural (his, her, their), the personal pronoun is invariable (i.e. the ending does not change with the gender of the word "possessed"). In the third person singular, there are separate pronouns for "his" and "her", but only one for "their" in the plural.

мой друг (m. sg.)	*moy drook*	my (male) friend
твоя подруга (f. sg.)	*tvaya padrooga*	my (female) friend
его друг (m. sg.)	*yivaw drook*	his (male) friend
её друг (m. sg.)	*yiyaw drook*	her (male) friend
наше такси (n. sg.)	*nashe taksi*	our taxi
ваши дети (m. pl.)	*vashee dyeti*	your children

SENTENCE STRUCTURE

The position of the words in a Russian sentence usually follows the following pattern: subject – verb – object. This sentence structure is found also in relative clauses (subordinate clauses in English, introduced by "which", "that", "whose", etc.) and even in questions (see **Questions**).

Subject	Verb	Object
doer	action	doee
Ольга	читает	журнал.
aw[ⱼ]ga	*chitayit*	*zhoornal*
Olga	reads	magazine

Olga is reading a/the magazine.

тридцать пять

Она	хочет читать	журнал.
ana	*khawchyit chita*t^s	*zhoorna*l
she	wants to-read	magazine

She wants to read a/the magazine.

These three core elements of a sentence (subject-vert-direct object) cannot be separated. For this reason, adverbs of time usually come at the beginning of the sentence and adverbs of place at the end:

When	Main action	Where
Сегодня	Ольга хочет читать журнал	дома.
syivawdnya	*awl*ly*ga khawchyit chita*t^s *zhoornal*	*dawma*
today	Olga wants to-read magazine	at-home

Today Olga wants to read a magazine at home.
or: Olga wants to read a magazine at home today.

In Russian, as in English, you can stress a word in a sentence by emphasizing its pronunciation.

VERBS

The Infinitive

The "basic form" of a verb consists of a stem plus an ending that indicates the infinitive form ("to do" form). The stem and the ending are separated by a hyphen in the examples below. The most common infinitive endings are **-ать/-ять** *at*^{s}*/yat*^{s}, and **-ить/-еть** *it*^{s}*/yet*^{s}. **-чь** *ch'* is less common.

The Present Tense

In English, there are two present tenses: the present continuous ("I am doing") and the simple present, which has two forms ("I do" and "I do do"). Luckily, Russian has only one form of the present tense to convey both those meanings.

	I. -е *ye* form	II. -ё *yaw* form	III. -и *i* form
	де́лать* d*ye*lat*s* to do/make	встава́ть fstavat*s* to get up	говори́ть gavarit*s* to speak/talk
я *ya*	де́ла<u>ю</u> d*ye*layoo	вста<u>ю́</u> fstayoo	говор<u>ю́</u> gavaryoo
ты *tee*	де́ла<u>ешь</u> d*ye*layish'	вста<u>ёшь</u> fstayawsh'	говор<u>и́шь</u> gavarish'
он, она́, оно́ *awn, ana, anaw*	де́ла<u>ет</u> d*ye*layit	вста<u>ёт</u> fstayawt	говор<u>и́т</u> gavarit
мы *mwee*	де́ла<u>ем</u> d*ye*layim	вста<u>ём</u> fstayawm	говор<u>и́м</u> gavarim
вы *vwee*	де́ла<u>ете</u> d*ye*layite	вста<u>ёте</u> fstayawtye	говор<u>и́те</u> gavaritye
они́ *ani*	де́ла<u>ют</u> d*ye*layoot	вста<u>ю́т</u> fstayoot	говор<u>я́т</u> gavaryat

* The present-tense ending is underlined.

To conjugate a verb in the present tense, you just have to recognize which group of verbs it belongs to:

• **Group I** (**-е** *ye* form): verbs whose infinitive ends in **-ать/ -ять** *at*s*/yat*s*, and whose last syllable is unstressed. To conjugate these verbs, drop the **-ть** *t*s* infinitive ending, and add the present-tense endings in **-е** *ye* after the final **-а** *a* or **-я** *ya* of the stem.

• **Group II** (**-ё** *yaw* form): verbs whose infinitive ends in **-ать/ -ять** *at*s*/yat*s*, and whose last syllable is stressed (underlined). To conjugate these verbs, drop the **-ть** *t*s* infinitive ending, and add the present-tense endings in **-ё** *yaw* after the final **-а** *a* or **-я** *ya* of the stem.

• **Group III** (**-и** *i* form): verbs whose infinitive ends in **-ить** *it*s*. To conjugate these verbs, drop the **-ть** *t*s* infinitive ending, and

тридцать семь

add the present-tense endings in **-и** *i* after the final consonant of the stem.

- Verbs whose infinitive ends in **-еть** *yet*ˢ are conjugated with endings in **-е** *ye* or **-и** *i*. The form to use is indicated in the English-Russian glossary at the back of the book.

- Verbs whose infinitive ends in **-овать** *ovat*ˢ and **-евать** *yevat*ˢ are conjugated with endings in **-е** *ye* but **-ова-** *ova* and **-ева-** *yeva* are replaced with **-у-** *oo*.

танцевать	tantsev<u>a</u>t^s	to dance
я танцую	ya tants<u>oo</u>yoo	I dance / am dancing
ты танцуешь	tee tants<u>oo</u>yish'	you dance / are dancing
они танцуют	ani tants<u>oo</u>yoot	they dance / are dancing

N.B. The present tense can only be formed from the "imperfective" (uncompleted action) infinitive. A completed action cannot be happening now.

If the same endings are used with "perfective" verbs (action that must be finished), the tense is future.

Aspect

Aspect is a grammatical feature of the Slavic languages. Russian aspect distinguishes between actions that are completed and are therefore irreversible (perfective aspect) and actions that are not yet complete or that could still continue (imperfective aspect). Consequently, most verbs have a "perfective" stem (perfect = complete) and an "imperfective" stem (not yet completed).
Recognizing the aspect of a verb makes it easier to understand a conversation. But your interlocutor will usually be able to guess what you mean from the context, even if you haven't chosen the right aspect. We suggest you stick to the imperfective at first, and only attempt "perfection" when your Russian is more advanced.

The Imperfective Aspect

> The imperfective denotes an action:
> • that is still continuing, or that lasted a certain amount of time.
> • that is repetitive, that recurs on a regular basis.

• Imperfective verbs can be conjugated in the present, the past and future tense.
• A sentence where English would use the present tense can only be translated into Russian with an imperfective verb.
• Time and frequency adverbs are usually associated with imperfective verbs:

всегда	fsyigda	always
ежедневно	yizheednyevna	every day
долго	dawlga	long time (for a ~)
часто	chasta	often
редко	ryetka	rarely
иногда	inagda	sometimes
сегодня	syivawdnya	today
обычно	abweechna	usually

Я работаю.
ya rabawtayoo
I work
I work (regularly).

Я читаю книгу.
ya chitayoo knigoo
I read book
I am reading a/the book.

Каждый день я делаю зарядку.
kazhdeey dyen[yi] ya dyelayoo zaryatkoo
every day I do exercise
I do (physical) exercises every day.

тридцать девять 39

The Perfective Aspect

> The perfective denotes an action whose result is known or that is limited in time. It is a single action:
> • that is completed/over.
> • that will definitely be completed/over in the future.

• Perfective verbs can only be conjugated in the past and future tense. They cannot be conjugated in the present tense because an action cannot be both in progress and already over. However, to conjugate perfective verbs in the future tense, the same endings as for the present-tense imperfective are used (see **The present tense**).

Мы проработали два часа.
mwee prarabawtali dva chisa
we worked-[perf.] two hours
We worked for two hours (... and finished!).

Я прочитаю книгу.
ya prachitayoo knigoo
I will-read-[perf.] book
I will read a/the book (... and finish it!).

МЫ ПРОРАБОТАЛИ ДВА ЧАСА.
(We worked for two hours.)

Вчера он сделал ошибку.
fchyira awn zdyelal asheepkoo
yesterday he made-[perf.] mistake
Yesterday he made a mistake (... only one!).

Perfective verbs are followed by [perf.] in the literal translations and the glossary. All verbs that do not have that indication are imperfective.

The Past Tense

English has a whole range of past tenses: the present perfect ("I have done"), the present perfect continuous ("I have been doing"), the past continuous ("I was doing"), the simple past, which has two forms ("I did" and "I did do"), the past perfect ("I had done") and the past perfect continuous ("I had been doing")! Luckily, Russian has only one past tense, which has only two forms: the perfective and the imperfective.

• To make things even easier, all verbs (both perfective and imperfective and regardless of their infinitive stem) have only two conjugations: the singular and the plural.

• However, in the singular, the ending changes depending on whether the subject is masculine, feminine or neuter.

• To conjugate a verb in the past tense, replace the infinitive ending **-ть** *t'* with one of the four possible past-tense endings:

Subject	Singular	Plural
masculine	**-л** *l*	
feminine	**-ла** *la*	**-ли** *li*
neuter	**-ло** *law*	

For example, the masculine singular past tense of **делать** *dyelat'*, *to do*, is **делал** *dyelal*, *I was doing / you were doing /*

he was doing. The masculine singular past tense of **говорить** *gavarit⁸, to speak,* is **говорил** *gavaril, I was speaking / you were speaking / he was speaking.*

Depending on the context, **он писал** *awn pisal* can be translated into English as *he has written,* or *he has been writing,* or *he was writing,* or *he wrote,* or *he had written,* or *he had been writing!*

Тамара писала письмо.
tamara pisala pisʸimaw
Tamara wrote-[f.] letter
Tamara was writing a/the letter.

Иван писал письмо.
ivan pisal pisʸimaw
Ivan wrote-[m.] letter
Ivan wrote a/the letter.

Тамара и Иван писали письмо.
tamara i ivan pisali pisʸimaw
Tamara and Ivan wrote-[pl.] letter
Tamara and Ivan had been writing a/the letter.

The Future Tense

The future tense of imperfective verbs describes an action that will start in the future (see **Aspect**). It is formed by using the auxiliary verb **быть** *bweet⁸, to be,* conjugated in the future, followed by the infinitive of the verb.

я буду	*ya boodoo*	I will be
ты будешь	*tee boodyish'*	you will be
он/она будет	*awn/ana boodyit*	he/she will be
мы будем	*mwee boodyim*	we will be
вы будете	*vwee boodyitye*	you will be
они будут	*ani boodoot*	they will be

Я буду учиться русскому языку.
ya boodoo oochitsa rooskamoo yizeekoo
I will-be to-learn-self Russian[3] language[3]
I will learn Russian.

The future tense of perfective verbs is formed by conjugating them the same way as the present tense of imperfective verbs (see **The imperfective aspect**). Compare the two future forms of the verb *to do*, the first in the imperfective: делать *dyelat͡s* and the second in the perfective: сделать *zdyelat͡s*:

Я буду делать.
ya boodoo dyelat͡s
I will-be to-do
I will do (probably).

Я сделаю.
ya zdyelayoo
I will-do
I will do (and I'll finish!).

Modal Verbs

Conjugating a verb in a foreign language is never easy. A smart way to get around the problem is to use modal verbs (want, can, must, etc.) plus the infinitive you want. It's a neat and handy way to avoid having to conjugate too many verbs.

For example, instead of asking, "Are you coming with us?", you could ask, "Do you want to / can you come with us?". This way, you only have to know how to conjugate about ten verbs and just know the infinitive of the others.

• Want, Like, Can, Be Able

	хотеть *khatyet͡s* to want	любить *lyoobit͡s* to like/love	мочь *mawch'* can	уметь *oomyet͡s* be able
я *ya*	хочу *khachoo*	люблю *lyooblyoo*	могу *magoo*	умею *oomyeyoo*
ты *tee*	хочешь *khawchyish'*	любишь *lyoobish'*	можешь *mawzhesh'*	умеешь *oomyeyish'*
он, она *awn, ana*	хочет *khawchyit*	любит *lyoobit*	может *mawzhet*	умеет *oomyeyit*
мы *mwee*	хотим *khatim*	любим *lyoobim*	можем *mawzhem*	умеем *oomyeyim*

сорок три

вы	хотите	любите	можете	умеете
vwee	khatityé	lyoobityé	mawzhetyé	oomyeyityé
они	хотят	любят	могут	умеют
an<u>i</u>	khat<u>ya</u>t	l<u>yoo</u>byat	m<u>aw</u>goot	oom<u>ye</u>yoot

Я хочу купить билеты.
ya khach<u>oo</u> koop<u>i</u>t⁵ bil<u>ye</u>tee
I want to-buy tickets
I want to buy some/the tickets.

Он хочет идти домой.
awn kh<u>aw</u>chyit itti dam<u>oy</u>
he wants to-go home
He wants to go home.

любить lyoob<u>i</u>t⁵, *to like/love* can be used by itself or as a modal auxiliary verb:

Я люблю путешествовать.
ya lyoobly<u>oo</u> pootyish<u>e</u>stvavat⁵
I like to-travel
I like travelling.

Я люблю слушать музыку.
ya lyoobly<u>oo</u> sl<u>oo</u>shat⁵ m<u>oo</u>zeekoo
I like to-listen music[4]
I like listening to music.

Я люблю тебя.
ya lyoobly<u>oo</u> tyib<u>ya</u>
I love you-[informal]
I love you.

Я люблю искусство.
ya lyoobly<u>oo</u> isk<u>oo</u>stva
I like art[4]
I like art.

Мочь mawch' means *to be able, to be allowed*. There is an irregular form, **можно** m<u>aw</u>zhna, *it is possible / it is allowed*, which is very common and easy to use:

Можно?
m<u>aw</u>zhna
May we? / May I?

Можно курить?
m<u>aw</u>zhna koor<u>i</u>t⁵
May we / May I smoke?

Можно войти?
mawzhna vayti
it-is-possible to-enter
May we / May I come in?

Можно! / Нельзя!
mawzhna / nyil[y]zya
it-is-possible / it-is-forbidden
Yes, you can! / No, you can't!

Где можно купить водку?
gdye mawzhna koopitˢ vawtkoo
where it-is-possible to-buy vodka[4]
Where can we buy vodka?

Уметь *oomyetˢ* means *to be able* in the sense of to be capable (physically or intellectually) of doing something. Note the difference between **уметь** *oomyetˢ*, *can / to be capable* and **мочь** *mawch'*, *can / to be allowed*.

Я умею плавать.
ya oomyeyoo plavatˢ
I can swim
I can / know how to swim.

Ты хорошо умеешь танцевать.
tee kharashaw oomyeyish' tantseevatˢ
you-[informal] well can to-dance
You're a good dancer.

• **Feel Like, Have To**

As well as conventional modal verbs, there are other constructions that are used in the same way, for example: **хочется** *khawchyitsa, to feel like,* and **надо** *nada, must,* preceded by a personal pronoun in the dative case and followed by a verb in the infinitive.

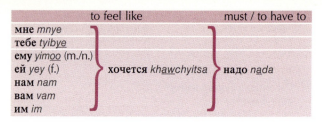

Мне хочется спать.
mnye kh<u>aw</u>chyitsa spat^s
to-me³ [it]-wants-self to-sleep
I want to sleep / feel like sleeping.

Ему хочется есть.
yim<u>oo</u> kh<u>aw</u>chyitsa yest^s
to-him³ [it]-wants-self to-eat
He wants to eat / feels like eating.

This construction is colloquial and is best only used with friends. In other cases, use the ordinary forms of the verb **хотеть** *khaty<u>et</u>^s*, *to want*, which are more correct.

Мне надо идти.
mnye n<u>a</u>da itt<u>i</u>
to-me³ it-is-necessary to-go
I have to go (leave now).

Надо *n<u>a</u>da*, *it is necessary*, is often used without a subject, with the verb in the infinitive. It means "this is the way things have to be done" and applies to everyone, including oneself:

Надо ждать.
n<u>a</u>da zhdat^s
it-is-necessary to-wait
You have to wait /
We all have to wait.

Надо пойти.
n<u>a</u>da payt<u>i</u>
it-is-necessary to-go
I have to go /
We all have to go.

The corresponding negative expression *you must not, we're not allowed, it is forbidden*, is **нельзя** *nyil^yzya*:

> **Здесь нельзя курить.**
> *zdyes^{yi} nyil^yzya koorit^s*
> here it-is-forbidden to-smoke
> You are not allowed to smoke here / Smoking prohibited.

• **Ought / Must / Have to / Should**

The verb **должен** *dawlzhen* is another way of expressing obligation. It is preceded by a personal pronoun (**я** *ya*, **ты** *tee*, **он** *awn*, **она** *ana*, **мы** *mwee*, **вы** *vwee*, **они** *ani*) and followed by a verb in the infinitive.

N.B. In the singular, **должен** *dawlzhen* agrees in gender (m., f., n.) with the subject; in the plural it is invariably **должны** *dalzhnee*.

	Singular	Plural
m.	должен *dawlzhen*	
f.	должна *dalzhna*	должны *dalzhnee*
n.	должно *dalzhnaw*	

> **Мы должны делать покупки.**
> *mwee dalzhnee dyelat^s pakoopki*
> we must to-do purchases
> We have to do the shopping.

> **Я должен уехать.**
> *ya dawlzhen ooyekhat^s*
> I must-[m.] to-leave-[by vehicle]
> I have to go.

> **Я должна уехать.**
> *ya dalzhna ooyekhat^s*
> I must-[f.] to-leave-[by vehicle]
> I have to go.

• **Need**

The adjective **нужен** *noozhen*, *necessary* is used to express someone's need for something. Where in English we say *I need something* or *I need to do something*, in Russian you use нужен _noozhen_ (lit. "is necessary") preceded by a personal pronoun in the dative case ("to me, to you", etc.) and followed by a noun or by a verb in the infinitive.

ЗДЕСЬ НЕЛЬЗЯ КУРИТЬ.
(No smoking.)

N.B. **Нужен** _noozheen_ does not agree with the subject, but with the needed object:

To be necessary	+	needed object
мне *mnye* тебе *tyibye* ему *yimoo* (m./n.) ей *yey* (f.) нам *nam* вам *vam* им *im*		нужен *noozhen* + m. sg. object нужна *noozhna* + f. sg. object нужно *noozhnaw* + n. sg. object нужны *noozhnee* + pl. object

Мне нужна виза.
mnye noozhna viza
to-me³ is-necessary-[f.] visa
I need a visa.

Мне нужны деньги.
mnye noozhnee dyen^ygi
to-me³ are-necessary money-[pl.]
I need money.

To Be and To Have

• **To Be**

As we have already seen, the verb "to be" is not conjugated in the present tense. Sentences that use the verb "to be" in the present tense in English have <u>no verb</u> in Russian (see chapter on ***Sentences without verbs***):

Он большой.
awn bal[y]sh<u>oy</u>
he big
He is big.

Она большая.
an<u>a</u> bal[y]sh<u>a</u>ya
she big
She is big.

• The only form of the verb "to be" used in the present tense is the invariable third person **есть** yest[s] meaning: *there is / there are*.

Есть ещё свободное место?
yest[s] yishch<u>yaw</u> svab<u>aw</u>dnaye m<u>ye</u>sta
there-is still free place
Are there any seats left?

The verb **быть** bweet[s], *to be*, is conjugated in the past and future. In the past, the singular forms only agree with the subject in gender (m., f., n.), not in person (I, you, he, etc.):

	Singular	Plural
m.	**был** bweel	
f.	**была** bwe<u>la</u>	**были** <u>bwee</u>li
n.	**было** <u>bwee</u>la	

Она была красивой.
an<u>a</u> bwe<u>la</u> kras<u>i</u>vay
she was beautiful
She was / used to be beautiful.

сорок девять

The future conjugations of the verb **быть** *bweet⁵*, *to be*, are given on page : ***The future***.

Это хорошо!
eta kharashaw
that good
That's good!

Это было хорошо!
eta bweela kharashaw
that was good
That was good!

Это будет хорошо!
eta boodyit kharashaw
that will-be good
That will be good!

- **To Have/Possess**

"To have" or "to possess" something is not translated by a verb as in English. Instead, a Russian says, "to me car", meaning that he owns a car or has a car. The Russian sentence uses the preposition **у** *oo*, *to* followed by a personal pronoun in the genitive case to express possession (on possession, see ***Case 2: the genitive***).

у *oo* + personal pronoun² = to me ᵍᵉⁿⁱᵗⁱᵛᵉ, to you ᵍᵉⁿⁱᵗⁱᵛᵉ, etc.

у меня	oo myinya	I have
у тебя	oo tyibya	you have
у него	oo nyivaw	he/it has
у неё	oo nyiyaw	she has
у нас	oo nas	we have
у вас	oo vas	you have
у них	oo nikh	they have

In the present tense, you can add **есть** *yest⁵* meaning *there is / there are* before the object to reinforce the idea of possession.

У меня есть машина.
oo myinya yest⁵ masheena
in-the-possession of-me² there-is car
I have/own a car.

Remember that **есть** *yest⁵* is invariable.

> **У нас есть дом.**
> *oo nas yest⁵ dawm*
> in-the-possession of-us² there-is house
> We have/own a house.

In the past, possession (I had / I owned) is expressed by adding the past-tense forms of the verb **быть** *bweet⁵*, *to be* (**был** *bweel*, *was*). N.B. **был** *bweel* agrees with the object owned, not with the owner.

> **У меня была машина.**
> *oo myinya bweela masheena*
> in-the-possession of-me² was-[f.] car-[f.]
> I had/owned a car.

> **У нас был дом.**
> *oo nas bweel dawm*
> in-the-possession of-us² was-[m.] house-[m.]
> We had/owned / used to have a house.

In the future, possession (I will have / I will own) is expressed by adding the future-tense forms of the verb **быть** *bweet⁵*, *to be*. If the object is singular, use the third-person singular form **будет** *boodyit*, *(he) will be*. If the object is plural, use the third-person plural form **будут** *boodoot*, *(they) will be*.

> **У неё будет брат.**
> *oo nyiyaw boodyit brat*
> in-the-possession of-her² will-be brother
> She is going to have a brother.

> **У меня будут каникулы.**
> *oo myinya boodoot kanikoolee*
> in-the-possession of-me² will-be-[pl.] holidays-[pl.]
> I will have holidays.

ПЯТЬДЕСЯТ ОДИН

Verbs of Motion

Like aspect (completed action versus action in progress), Russian makes a distinction between "unidirectional" and "multidirectional" movement (or "precise" and "vague" movement). Verbs of motion therefore come in pairs. The type of movement determines which verb in the pair will be used:

Unidirectional verbs describe movement that is:
- a single journey;
- with a precise direction or goal;
- occurring within a defined time.

Multidirectional verbs describe movement that is:
- regular;
- with no precise goal (back and forth, round and round, etc.);
- habitual (even if there is a direction and goal);
- possible, general.

The most common pairs are:

	Unidirectional	Multidirectional
to go (on foot)	идти *itti*	ходить *khadit^s*
to go (by vehicle)	ехать *yekhat^s*	ездить *yezdit^s*
to fly	лететь *lyityet^s*	летать *lyitat^s*
to swim	плыть *pleet^s*	плавать *plavat^s*
to carry/bring (on foot)	нести *nyisti*	носить *nasit^s*

Unidirectional:

Сегодня я иду в театр.
syivawdnya ya idoo f-tyiatr
today I go-on-foot to theater
I am going to the theater today.

Multidirectional:

Я часто хожу в театр.
ya chasta khazhoo f-tyiatr
I often go-on-foot to theater
I often go to the theater.

Мы едем на выставку.
mwee yedyim na vweestafkoo
we go-by-vehicle to exhibition
We're going to an/the exhibition.

Он ездит на пляж.
awn yezdit na plyash
he goes-by-vehicle to beach
He goes to the beach (often, sometimes).

Он идёт домой.
awn idyawt damoy
he goes-on-foot home
He is going home.

Он ходит по двору.
awn khawdyit pa-dvaroo
he goes-on-foot by courtyard
He is walking around the courtyard.

("Unidirectional" verbs are followed by (unidir.) in the glossary at the back of the book).

Reflexive Verbs

Reflexive verbs, where the action is turned back on the subject (and is done either "to oneself" or "to each other") are easily recognisable in the infinitive by the ending **-ся** *sa*, *self*. They are easy to form from non-reflexive verbs, when a reflexive meaning makes sense:

развлекать	*razvlyikat^s*	to entertain
развлекаться	*razvlyikatsa*	to enjoy oneself / have fun
знакомить	*znakawmit^s*	to introduce (people)
знакомиться	*znakawmitsa*	to get to know (each other)
встретить	*fstryetit^s*	to meet
встретиться	*fstryetitsa*	to meet (each other)
занимать	*zanimat^s*	to occupy
заниматься	*zanimatsa*	to occupy oneself, to do

N.B. The meaning of the reflexive form (with **-ться** *tsa*) is sometimes completely unrelated to the non-reflexive form (without **-ться** *tsa*).

пятьдесят три

договаривать *dagavarivat*ˢ to finish talking	but...	договариваться *dagavarivatsa* to agree
прощать *prashchat*ˢ to forgive	but...	прощаться *prashchatsa* to say goodbye/farewell

Unlike Russian, English does not have a grammatical reflexive form. The concept of reflexive verbs can take a little getting used to. It is obvious in some cases, less in others.

учиться	*oochitsa*	to learn
начинаться	*nachinatsa*	to begin

Reflexive verbs are conjugated in exactly the same way as the non-reflexive form, simply by adding **-ся** after consonants and **-сь** after vowels.

встречаться	*fstryichatsa*	to meet (each other)
я встречаю<u>сь</u>	*ya fstryichayoos*ʸⁱ	
ты встречае<u>шься</u>	*tee fstryichayish'sya*	
он/она встречае<u>тся</u>	*awn/ana fstryichayitsa*	
мы встречае<u>мся</u>	*mwee fstryichayemsya*	
вы встречае<u>тесь</u>	*vwee fstryichayityes*ʸⁱ	
они встречаю<u>тся</u>	*ani fstryichayootsa*	

The same construction applies to the past tense:

	Singular	Plural
	я, ты, он/она *ya, tee, awn/ana*	мы, вы, они *mwee, vwee, ani*
m.	встреча<u>лся</u> *fstryichalsya*	
f.	встреча<u>лась</u> *fstryichalas*ʸⁱ	встреча<u>лись</u> *fstryichalis*ʸⁱ
n.	встреча<u>лось</u> *fstryichalas*ʸⁱ	

To conjugate a reflexive verb in the future tense, you usually just use the auxiliary verb **быть** bweet^s, *to be*, conjugated in the future followed by the reflexive verb in the infinitive (**-ся** *sa*):

> **Я буду встречаться с друзьями.**
> *ya boodoo fstryichatsa z-drooz^{y¦}yami*
> I will-be to-meet-self with friends
> I am going to meet some friends.

Note that **-ся** is pronounced *sa* after **у**, **ю**, **т**, **ть** and **л** (the first person singular, third person singular and plural, and the infinitive and masculine past forms). After **шь**, **е**, **м** and **а** (the second person singular and plural, first person plural and imperative forms) it is pronounced *sya*.

Irregular Verbs

Russian irregular verbs are partly regular! Most of the conjugation endings are regular, but the stem changes in some tenses and persons. The glossary at the back of the book gives the irregular verb forms. There are two main groups of irregular verbs:

- Group 1: the stem changes only in the first person singular ("I") in the present tense. All the other persons are regular. Most verbs in this group have an infinitive in **-ить** *it^s*.
- Group 2: the stem changes in the present tense (it is different from the infinitive stem), but the endings are regular.

	Group 1 **ходить** *khadit^s* (to go on foot)	Group 2 **ехать** *yekhat^s* (to go by vehicle)
я *ya*	**хожу** *khazhoo*	**еду** *yedoo*
ты *tee*	**ходишь** *khawdish'*	**едешь** *yedyish'*
он/она *awn/ana*	**ходит** *khawdit*	**едет** *yedyit*

мы twee	ходим kh<u>aw</u>dim	едем y<u>e</u>dyim
вы vwee	ходите kh<u>aw</u>ditye	едете y<u>e</u>dyitye
они an<u>i</u>	ходят kh<u>aw</u>dyat	едут y<u>e</u>doot

N.B. The unidirectional verb идти *itti*, *to go on foot*, is irregular in the past tense: шёл *shawl* (m. sg.) / шла *shla* (f. sg.) / шли *shli* (pl.).

The Imperative

The imperative is the verb form used for commands. The singular, familiar, imperative is used for a person you address as **ты** *tee*, and the plural for a person you address as **вы** *vwee* or when addressing more than one person. The imperative is formed from the stem of the third person plural. To obtain the stem, remove the ending (-**ят** *yat* / -**ат** *at* or -**ют** *yoot* / -**ут** *oot*). For example, the stem of the verb "to do" is obtained from **они делают** *an<u>i</u> dy<u>e</u>layoot*, *they do*, and is thus **дела** *dyil<u>a</u>*. Then you just have to add the relevant imperative endings to that stem:

Stem ending in a...	vowel	consonant
• imperative singular	-й *y*	-и *i*
• imperative plural (and polite you form)	-йте *ytye*	-ите *itye*

они делают	*an<u>i</u> dy<u>e</u>layoot*	they do
Делай!	*dy<u>e</u>lay*	Do! (you sg. informal)
Делайте!	*dy<u>e</u>laytye*	Do! (you sg. formal / plural)
они говорят	*an<u>i</u> gavary<u>a</u>t*	they speak
Говори!	*gavar<u>i</u>*	Speak! (you sg. informal)
Говорите!	*gavar<u>i</u>tye*	Speak! (you sg. formal / plural)

In the literal translation, verbs in the imperative are indicated by an exclamation mark in square brackets [!].

Дайте мне, пожалуйста, книгу!
daytye mnye pazhalsta knigoo
give-[!]-[formal/plural] to-me³ please book
Give me the book, please!

Помоги / Помогите мне!
pamagi / pamagitye mnye
help-[!]-[informal] / help-[!]-[formal/plural] to-me³
Help me!

Подождите минутку!
padazhditye minootkoo
wait-[!]-[formal/plural] little-minute⁴
Wait a minute!

Повторите, пожалуйста, это слово!
paftaritye pazhalsta eta slawva
repeat-[!]-[formal/plural] please that word
Could you repeat that word, please?

Иди сюда!
idi syooda
come-[!]-[informal]
Come here!

Идите сюда!
iditye syooda
come-[!]-[formal/plural]
Come here!

Входи!
fkhadi
come-in-[!]-[informal]
Come in!

Входите!
fkhaditye
come-in-[!]-[formal/plural]
Come in!

Direct imperatives are less common in English, which prefers introductory constructions like "can you...?" or "could you...?". Even in Russian, imperatives will be better received if you add **пожалуйста** *pazhalsta*, *please*:

Прости/Простите, пожалуйста, ...!
prasti/prastitye pazhalsta
forgive-[!]-[informal]/forgive-[!]-[formal/plural] please
Excuse me, ...

Извини/Извините, пожалуйста, …!
izvini/izvinitye pazhalsta
excuse-[!]-[informal]/excuse-[!]-[formal/plural] please
Excuse me, …

ИЗВИНИТЕ!
(Sorry!)

Скажи/Скажите, пожалуйста, …!
skazhee/skazheetye pazhalsta
say-[!]-[informal]/say-[!]-[formal/plural] please
Can you tell me, please…?

Покажи/Покажите, пожалуйста, …!
pakazhee/pakazheetye pazhalsta
show-[!]-[informal]/show-[!]-[formal/plural] please
Can you show me, please…?

Разреши/Разрешите, пожалуйста, …!
razryishee/razryisheetye pazhalsta
permit-[!]-[informal]/permit-[!]-[formal/plural] please
Allow me, please…

CONJUNCTIONS

Conjunctions (linking words) are used in the same way as in English:

и	*i*	and
потому что	*pata<u>moo</u>-shta*	because
а, но	*a, naw*	but
или... или	*<u>i</u>li... <u>i</u>li*	either... or
как	*kak*	how, as
если	*<u>ye</u>sli*	if
ни... ни	*ni... ni*	neither... nor
или	*<u>i</u>li*	or
чтобы	*sht<u>aw</u>bwee*	so that / in order to
что	*shtaw*	that
тогда	*tagd<u>a</u>*	then / in that case
потом	*pat<u>aw</u>m*	then / afterwards
поэтому	*pa<u>e</u>tamoo*	therefore / for that reason
когда	*kagd<u>a</u>*	when

Он сказал, что он придёт сегодня.
awn skaz<u>a</u>l shtaw awn prid<u>yaw</u>t syiv<u>aw</u>dnya
he said that he will-come today
He said he would come today.

Или сегодня или завтра придёт моя семья.
<u>i</u>li syiv<u>aw</u>dnya <u>i</u>li z<u>a</u>ftra prid<u>yaw</u>t maya syim'ya
or today or tomorrow will-come my family
My family is coming today or tomorrow.

Идите прямо, а потом налево!
id<u>i</u>tye pry<u>a</u>ma a pat<u>aw</u>m nal<u>ye</u>va
go-[!] straight and then left
Go straight and then left!

пятьдесят девять 59

THE SIX CASES

In Russian, common nouns, adjectives, pronouns and numbers all decline. That means that the ending of the word changes depending on its function in the sentence (subject, object, indirect object, etc.).
This chapter will only deal with declensions of nouns and adjectives.

There are six cases in Russian:

Case	Answers question
1. nominative (subject)	Who? What?
2. genitive (possessive)	Whose? Of What? From where?
3. dative (indirect object)	To whom? To what?
4. accusative (direct object)	Whom? What? Where to?
5. instrumental (by means of which)	With whom? With what? By means of what?
6. locative (location)	Where? In which place?

My brother's[2] son[1] lives in Moscow[6]. He came with his wife[5] to give my mother[3] a gift[4].

In the previous example, numbers are used to indicate the cases the nouns would take in Russian. Each case reflects a different function in the sentence. The literal translations also show case numbers.

Case 1: The Nominative

The nominative case denotes the subject of the action. It is also the basic or "undeclined" case, in which nouns and adjectives appear in the dictionary. The nouns and adjectives in the glossary at the back of the book are all in the nominative case.

Case 2: The Genitive

The genitive case denotes possession or a relationship between two objects/people. Russian uses the genitive where English uses the preposition "of" or the possessive "'s":

машина друга
masheena drooga
car of-friend[2]
a/the friend's car

книга подруги
kniga padroogi
book of-girlfriend[2]
a/the girlfriend's book

The genitive case is also used after some numbers and expressions of quantity (see **Numbers**).

три килограмма
tri kilagramma
three of-kilogram[2]
three kilograms

пять литров бензина
pyat[s] litraf byinzina
five of-liters[2] of-gasoline[2]
five liters of gasoline

Сколько литров?
skawl[y]ka litraf
how-many of-liters[2]
How many liters?

несколько друзей
nyeskal[y]ka droozyey
a-few of-friends[2]
a few friends

много туристов
mnawga tooristaf
many of-tourists[2]
many tourists

The genitive also denotes geographical origin. Proper nouns (place names) decline too.

Откуда вы?
atkooda vwee
from-where you-[formal/plural]
Where are you from?

Я из (города) Вашингтона.
ya iz (gawrada) vashinktawna
I from (city[2]) Washington[2]
I'm from (the city of) Washington.

Some conjunctions are always followed by the genitive case, such as **из** *iz* and **от** *awt*, *from*; **до** *daw*, *up to* and **у** *oo*, *at someone's place*.

От Москвы до Новгорода
at maskv<u>wee</u> da n<u>aw</u>vgarada
from Moscow[2] to Novgorod[2]
from Moscow to Novgorod

У меня
oo myin<u>ya</u>
at-the-place of-me[2]
at my place

Case 3: The Dative

The dative case is used for indirect objects and answers the question "to whom?". For example, after verbs like "to write", "to give", "to say". Russian uses the dative where English uses the preposition "to":

Я дал/дала другу книгу
ya dal/dal<u>a</u> dr<u>oo</u>goo kn<u>i</u>goo
I gave-[m./f.] to-friend[3] book[4]
I gave the book to a friend.

Я пишу подруге
ya pish<u>oo</u> padr<u>oo</u>gi
I am-writing to-girlfriend[3]
I am writing to a girlfriend.

Case 4: The Accusative

The accusative case is used for direct objects and answers the question "whom?" or "what?" (What is he watching? What is he reading?):

Я вижу друга.
ya v<u>i</u>zhoo dr<u>oo</u>ga
I see friend[4]
I can see a friend.

Я написал/написала открытку.
ya napisal/napisal<u>a</u> atkr<u>ee</u>tkoo
I wrote-[m./f.] postcard[4]
I wrote a postcard.

Он читает книгу.
awn chit<u>a</u>yit kn<u>i</u>goo
he is-reading book[4]
He is reading a book.

Он читает книги.
awn chit<u>a</u>yit kn<u>i</u>gi
he is-reading books[4]
He reads books.

In Russian, destinations are also in the accusative when there is movement towards them:

Я еду в Москву.
ya yedoo v-maskvoo
I am-going-by-vehicle to Moscow[4]
I am going to Moscow.

Я еду в (город) Вашингтон.
ya yedoo v (gawrad) vashinktawn
I am-going-by-vehicle to (city[4]) Washington[4]
I am going to (the city of) Washington.

Case 5: The Instrumental

The instrumental case denotes the instrument! It is used for words that answer the question "with whom?" or "with what?". It is also used after some verbs, like **заниматься** *zanimatsa, to do* (lit. "to occupy self with") and after some conjunctions:

Я занимаюсь музыкой.
ya zanimayoos^yi moozeekay
I occupy-self music[5]
I play music.

Я говорю с другом.
ya gavarayoo z-droogam
I talk with friend[5]
I am talking to a friend.

Case 6: The Locative

The locative case answers the question "where?", but only when there is no movement. Words in the locative case always come after a preposition (at, in, etc.).

Я живу в Америке.
ya zheevoo v-amyerikye
I live in America[6]
I live in America.

Я был/была в школе.
ya bweel/bweela f-shkawlye
I was-[m./f.] at school[6]
I was at school.

шестьдесят три

В городе есть кино.
v-gawradye yestˢ kinaw
in town⁶ there-is cinema
There is a movie theater in town.

Он рассказывает о каникулах.
awn raskazeevayit a kanikoolakh
he tells about vacation⁶
He is telling [people] about his vacation.

DECLENSIONS

Declension of Common Nouns

Declensions of nouns are quite complicated! Russian not only has three genders (masculine, feminine and neuter), it also makes a distinction between living beings and things (animate and inanimate) and between nouns with a hard ending (e.g. **-а** *a*) and those with a soft ending (e.g. **-я** *ya*) in the nominative case.

In the tables below, we have tried to simplify things as much as possible. For example, the table contains only hard-ending nouns (with one exception).

To highlight the declensions, the endings are underlined in the tables.

• Singular Declensions

Masculine inanimate	Masculine animate	Feminine	Feminine in **-ь** ˢ	Neuter
театр	брат	комната	тетрадь	место
tyiatr	*brat*	*kawmnata*	*tyitratˢ*	*myesta*
theater	brother	room	notebook	place

	Masculine		Feminine	Feminine in -ь	Neuter
1. N	театр tyiatr	брат brat	комната kawmnata	тетрадь tyitrat^s	место myesta
2. G	театра tyiatra	брата brata	комнаты kawmnatee	тетради tyitradi	места myesta
3. D	театру tyiatroo	брату bratoo	комнате kawmnatye	тетради tyitradi	месту myestoo
4. A	театр tyiatr	брата brata	комнату kawmnat oo	тетрадь tyitrat^s	место myesta
5. I	театром tyiatram	братом bratam	комнатой kawmnatay	тетрадью tyitrat^syoo	местом myestam
6. L	театре tyiatrye	брате bratye	комнате kawmnatye	тетради tyitradi	месте myestye

N.B. In the masculine singular, the only difference between animate and inanimate is in the accusative case (case 4). In the accusative:
- Animate masculine nouns decline like the genitive (case 2).
- Inanimate masculine nouns stay like the nominative (case 1).

• **Plural Declensions**

	Masculine	Feminine	Feminine in -ь	Neuter
	театры tyiatree theaters	комнаты kawmnatee rooms	тетради tyitradi notebooks	места myista places
1. N	театры tyiatree	комнаты kawmnatee	тетради tyitradi	места myista
2. G	театров tyiatraf	комнат kawmnat	тетрадей tyitradyey	мест myest
3. D	театрам tyiatram	комнатам kawmnatam	тетрадям tyitradyam	местам myistam
4. A	(1. or 2.)	(1. or 2.)	(1. or 2.)	места myista
5. I	театрами tyiatrami	комнатами kawmnatami	тетрадями tyitradyami	местами myistami
6. L	театрах tyiatrakh	комнатах kawmnatakh	тетрадях tyitradyakh	местах myistakh

- Whatever the gender, for inanimate nouns (things), Case 4 is the same as Case 1 (as in the four examples above). For animate nouns (living beings), Case 4 is the same as Case 2!
- Hard-ending feminine nouns have no ending in the genitive plural (Case 2).

Declension of Soft-Ending Nouns

Soft-ending nouns (see **Gender**) usually decline like hard-ending nouns of the same gender. The only difference is that the vowel softens:

Hard ending	becomes	Soft ending
-а *a*		-я *ya*
-ов *awv*		-ев *yev*
-у *oo*		-ю *yoo*
-о *aw*		-е *ye*
-ом *awm*		-ем *yem*
-ой *oy*		-ей *yey*
-ами *ami*		-ями *yami*
-ы *ee*		-и *i*
-ах *akh*		-ях *yakh*

- An exception to this rule is feminine nouns ending in a syllable with **-ь** (see their declension, **Singular/Plural declensions**).
- Handy hint: if you are unsure of the declension of a word, don't decline it (leave it in the nominative). That is better than getting the wrong declension.

Declension of Personal Pronouns

In English, we decline personal pronouns, often without even realizing it. We don't say "I'll call he", but "I'll call him". Russian also declines personal pronouns in the same six cases as nouns. On the previous pages, you have already encountered the following cases:

- Case 2 (G): **(у) меня** *(oo) myinya*, **(у) тебя** *(oo) tyibya*, in my/your possession or at my/your place.
- Case 3 (D): **мне** *mnye*, **тебе** *tyibye*, to me/you.
- Case 4 (A): same as Case 2.

In the table below, only the Case 5 and 6 declensions are new to you:

	я *ya* I	**ты** *tee* you	**он** *awn* he **оно** *anaw* it	**она** *ana* she
2. + 4. G + A	**меня** *myinya*	**тебя** *tyibya*	**его** *yivaw*	**её** *yiyaw*
3. D	**мне** *mnye*	**тебе** *tyibye*	**ему** *yimoo*	**ей** *yey*
5. I	**мной** *tnoy*	**тобой** *taboy*	**(н)им** *(n)im*	**(н)ею** *(n)yeyoo*
6. L	**мне** *mnye*	**тебе** *tyibye*	**нём** *nyawm*	**ней** *nyey*

	мы *mwee* we	**вы** *vwee* you	**они** *ani* they	**себя** *syibya* myself, yourself, ... themselves
2. + 4. G + A	**нас** *nas*	**вас** *vas*	**их** *ikh*	**себя** *syibya*
3. D	**нам** *nam*	**вам** *vam*	**им** *im*	**себе** *syibye*
5. I	**нами** *nami*	**вами** *vami*	**(н)ими** *(n)imi*	**собой** *saboy*
6. L	**нас** *nas*	**вас** *vas*	**них** *nikh*	**себе** *syibye*

Я тебя люблю.
ya tyibya lyooblyoo
I you[4]-[informal] love
I love you.

Это мне очень нравится.
eta mnye awchyin[yi] nravitsa
that to-me[3] very pleases-self
I really like that.

Here are some standard expressions:

мы с тобой
mwee s-taboy
we with you[5]-[informal]
you and I

мы с вами
mwee s-vami
we with you[5]-[formal/plural]
you and we

про себя
pra syibya
for self[2]
to oneself / silently

у себя
oo syibya
at-the-place of-self[2]
at home

If the pronoun beginning with a vowel comes after a word ending in a vowel, an **н-** *n* is added to the beginning of the pronoun, to avoid having to pronounce a vowel after another vowel. We do something similar in English when we say "an apple" instead of "a apple".

у него
oo nyivaw
at-the-place of-him[2]
he has / at his place

у неё
oo nyiyaw
at-the-place of-her[2]
she has / at her place

между ними
myezhdoo nimi
among them[5]
among themselves

Себя *syibya*, *self*, is used wherever English would say *myself, yourself, himself,* etc. Compare the sentences below:

Он купил мне книгу.
awn koopil mnye knigoo
he bought-[m.] for-me[3] book[4]
He bought a/the book for me.

Я купил/купила себе книгу.
ya koopil/koopila syibye knigoo
I bought-[m./f.] for-self[3] book[4]
I bought myself a/the book.

NEGATION

Нет and *Не*

To negate a sentence, simply insert **не** *nyi/nye*, *not*, in front of the verb. The rest of the sentence stays the same. To emphasize the negation, place **нет** *nyet*, *no*, at the beginning of the sentence:

Нет, я не понимаю.
nyet ya nyi panim<u>a</u>yoo
no I not understand
No, I don't understand.

я не получал/получала письмо.
ya nyi palooch<u>a</u>l/palooch<u>a</u>la pis^yj<u>maw</u>
I not received-[m./f.] letter⁴
I didn't receive the letter.

Да нет!
da nyet
yes no
Of course not!

Комната мне не нравится.
k<u>aw</u>mnata mnye nyi nr<u>a</u>vitsa
room to-me not likes-self
I don't like the room.

Sentences with the words below must also contain **не** *nyi* or **нет** *nyet*, *not*. This "double negative" is the correct form in Russian!

никогда	nikagd<u>a</u>	never
никто, никого	nikt<u>aw</u>, nikav<u>aw</u>	no one
ничто, ничего	nisht<u>aw</u>, nichiv<u>aw</u>	nothing
нигде	nigd<u>ye</u>	nowhere (in ~)
никуда	nikood<u>a</u>	nowhere (to ~)

Ничего не поделаешь!
nichiv<u>aw</u> nyi pady<u>e</u>layish'
nothing not [you-formal/plural]-will-do-[perf.]
There's nothing you can do!

Ничего нет.
nichiv<u>aw</u> nyet
nothing no
No harm done.

Я никого не видел/видела.
ya nikav<u>aw</u> nyi v<u>i</u>dyil/v<u>i</u>dyila
I no-one not saw-[m./f.]
I haven't seen anyone / didn't see anyone.

шестьдесят девять

Нигде не мог/могла купить пиво.

nigdye nyi mawk/magla koopit⁵ piva
nowhere not could-[m./f.] to-buy beer²
I couldn't buy beer anywhere.

In colloquial Russian, **Ничего!** *nichyivaw* means *It doesn't matter!*

Negation of *Есть*

To express the idea of "don't have" / "there isn't" in the present tense, Russian uses **нет** *nyet*, *there is not*, with the object in the genitive case (Case 2).

This is the negative form of sentences with **есть** *yest⁵*, *there is*, in Russian.

Нигде нет хлеба.	**У меня нет времени.**
nigdye nyet khlyeba	*oo myinya nyet vryemyini*
nowhere not bread²	in-the-possession of-me² no time²
There's no bread anywhere.	I don't have time.

To express the idea of "didn't have" / "there wasn't" in the past tense, Russian uses **не** *nyi*, *not*, with **было** *bweela*, *there was not*, and the object in the genitive case (Case 2).

Нигде не было хлеба.

nigdye nyi bweela khlyeba
nowhere not was-[n.] bread²
There was no bread anywhere.

To express the idea of "will not have" / "there won't be" in the future tense, Russian uses **не** *nyi*, *not* with **будет** *boodyit*, *there will not be* and the object in the genitive case (Case 2).

У меня не будет времени.

oo myinya nyi boodyit vryemyini
in-the-possession of-me² not it-will-be time²
I won't have time.

PREPOSITIONS CASE BY CASE

As you have probably noticed in the examples so far, the words that come after prepositions take different cases. The tables below show common prepositions and the cases they govern.

N.B. Some prepositions have more than one meaning and therefore govern more than one case. These prepositions appear in more than one table.

To help you understand this chapter, we recommend you read the description of the cases again.

Prepositions that Take the Genitive (Case 2)

после	_paw_slye	after (time)
против	_praw_tif	against, opposite
около	_aw_kala	around, near (a place)
у	oo	at, at the place of
кроме	_kraw_mye	except, apart from
для	dlya	for
из	iz/is	from (a place), because of (something)
от	awt/at	from (a place)
с	s	from (a place), from (a time) onwards
вместо	_vmye_sta	instead of
до	daw/da	up to (a place), until (a time)
без	biz/bis	without

с утра
s-oo_tra_
from morning[2]
from the morning onwards

до отхода поезда
da-atkh_aw_da p_aw_yizda
until departure[2] of-train[2]
until the train leaves

у родителей
oo radityelyey
at-the-place of-parents[2]
at (my) parents'

Prepositions that Take the Dative (Case 3)

по	*paw/pa*	by, according to, along
благодаря	*blagadarya*	thanks to, depending on
к	*k*	to (a direction), to someone's place

Мы гуляли по улицам.
mwee goolyali pa-oolitsam
we walked along streets[3]
We wandered the streets.

Я иду к другу.
ya idoo k-droogoo
I go to-the-place of-friend[3]
I'm going to my friend's place.

Prepositions that Take the Accusative (Case 4)

на	*na*	in (a place), to (a place), for (a time)
через	*chyiryiz*	through, across, over, in (a period of time)
в	*v/f*	to (a place), in/on (a time)
по	*paw/pa*	until the end of

через улицу
chyiryiz-oolitsoo
across street[4]
across the street

через два часа
chyiryiz-dva chisa
through two of-hour[2]
in two hours' time

Я еду в Москву.
ya yedoo v-maskvoo
I go-by-vehicle to Moscow[4]
I am driving to Moscow.

в среду
f-sryedoo
on Wednesday[4]
on Wednesday

Я кладу книгу на стол.
ya kladoo knigoo na stawl
I put book[4] on table[4]
I am putting the book on the table.

по июль
pa-iyool[yi]
until-the-end-of July[4]
until the end of July

Prepositions that Take the Instrumental (Case 5)

над	*nad/nat*	above
между	*myezhdoo*	between, among
перед	*pyiryid*	in front of
с	*s*	with

перед домом
pyiryid dawmam
in-front-of house[5]
in front of the/a house

Лампа висит над столом.
lampa visit nat-stalawm
light hangs above table[5]
The light hangs above the table.

между народами
myezhdoo narawdami
between peoples[5]
between/among peoples

с подругой/другом
s-padroogay/droogam
with girlfriend/friend[5]
with a (girl)friend

Prepositions that Take the Locative (Case 6)

о	*aw/a*	about
при	*pri*	beside, during
в	*v/f*	in/at (a place), in (a time)
на	*na*	on

При доме находится сад.
pri dawmye nakhawditsa sat
beside house[6] finds-self garden
Beside the house is a garden.

Он живёт в Москве.
awn zheevyawt v-maskvye
he lives in Moscow[6]
He lives in Moscow.

Петербург стоит на Неве.
pyityirboork stait na nyivye
Petersburg stands on Neva[6]
Saint-Petersburg lies on the Neva.

Я учусь в университете.
ya ooch<u>oo</u>s^{yi} v-oonivyirsit<u>ye</u>tye
I learn-self at university[6]
I am studying at university.

When the word that comes after the preposition starts with two consonants, **-o** *o/a* is added to some prepositions. For example:

во всех странах мира
va vsyekh stran<u>a</u>kh m<u>i</u>ra
in all[6] countries[6] of-world[2]
in all countries of the world

QUESTIONS

Closed Questions

A question that can be answered **да** *da*, *yes*, or **нет** *nyet*, *no* is called a "closed" question.

Questions in Russian keep the same word order as statements. Questions are pronounced with extra emphasis on the key word.

Поезд ушёл?	**Да, поезд ушёл.**
p<u>aw</u>yist oosh<u>aw</u>l	*da p<u>aw</u>yist oosh<u>aw</u>l*
train left	yes train left
Has the train left?	Yes, the train has left.
Он был в театре?	**Да, он был в театре.**
awn bweel f-tyi<u>a</u>trye	*da awn bweel f-tyi<u>a</u>trye*
he was-[m.] at theater	yes he was-[m.] at theater
Was he at the theater?	Yes, he was at the theater.

It is also common to answer a closed question by repeating the emphasized key word or words, with or without **да** *da*, *yes* or **нет** *nyet*, *no*.

Он <u>был</u> в театре?
awn bweel f-tyiatrye
he was-[m.] at theater
Was he at the theater?

Да, был.
da bweel
yes was-[m.]
Yes, he was.

Нет, не был.
nyet nyi bweel
no not was-[m.]
No, he wasn't.

Он был <u>в театре</u>?
awn bweel f-tyiatrye
he was-[m.] at theater
Was he at the theater?

Да, в театре.
da f-tyiatrye
yes at theater
Yes, he was at the theater.

Нет, в зоопарке.
nyet v-zaaparkye
no at zoo
No, he was at the zoo.

ПОЕЗД УШЁЛ?
(Has the train left?)

Another way of forming questions is to invert the subject and verb, as in English. In this case, the particle **ли** *li* must be inserted between the verb and the subject. However, this is a very formal construction, which is rarely used.

> **Пойдёте ли вы...?**
> *paydyawtye-li vwee*
> go [question-word] you-[formal/plural]
> Are you going...?

People would usually say:

> **Вы пойдёте...?**
> *vwee paydyawtye*
> you-[formal/plural] go
> Are you going… ?

Open Questions

Open questions are all questions that can't simply be answered yes or no. e.g. What can you say in Russian? Open questions begin with an interrogative pronoun (question word):

Как?	kak	How?
Сколько раз?	skawl[y]ka ras	How many times?
Сколько?	skawl[y]ka	How much/many?
Когда?	kagda	When?
С каких пор?	s-kakikh pawr	When (since ~ ?)
Где?	gdye	Where?
Откуда?	atkooda	Where from?
Куда?	kooda	Where to ?
У кого?	oo kavaw	Whose? / At whose place?
Почему?	pachyimoo	Why?

- N.B. **Сколько** *skawl[y]ka* governs the genitive case!

Сколько людей?
skawl[y]ka lyoodyey
how-many of-people[2]
How many people?

The interrogative adjective **какой** kakoy, *which*, like other adjectives, agrees in gender in the singular and has a "unisex" form in the plural:

Какой (m.)	**Какая** (f.)	**Какое** (n.)	**Какие** (pl.)
kakoy	*kakaya*	*kakoye*	*kakiye*
Which?	Which?	Which?	Which?

Какой человек?
kakoy chyilavyek
Which man?

Какая женщина?
kakaya zhenshchina
Which woman?

The interrogative pronouns **Кто?** *ktaw*, *Who?* and **Что?** *shtaw*, *What?* decline.

1. **Кто?** *ktaw* Who?	**Что?** *shtaw* What?
2. **Кого?** *kavaw* Of whom/whose?	**Чего?** *chyivaw* Of what?
3. **Кому?** *kamoo* To whom?	**Чему?** *chyimoo* To what?
4. **Кого?** *kavaw* Whom?	**Что?** *shtaw* What?
5. **С кем?** *s-kyem* With whom?	**С чем?** *s-chyem* With what?
6. **О ком?** *a-kawm* About whom?	**О чём?** *a chyawm* About what?

Куда ведёт эта дорога?
kooda vyidyawt eta darawga
to-where leads this road
Where does this road lead?

Где находится собор?
gdye nakhawditsa sabor
where finds-self cathedral
Where is the cathedral?

Как пройти на почту?
kak prayti na pawchtoo
how to-go-through to post-office
How do I get to the post office?

У кого есть два лишних билета?
oo kav*aw* yest⁶ dva l*i*shnikh bil*ye*ta
at whose² there-is two spare² ticket²
Who has two spare tickets?

Когда начинается представление?
kagd*a* nachin*ay*itsa pryidstavl*ye*niye
when starts-self performance
When does the performance start?

Когда вы идёте домой?
kagd*a* vwee id*yaw*tye dam*oy*
when you-[formal/plural] go home
When are you going home?

Куда вы едете?
kood*a* vwee *ye*dyitye
to-where you-[formal/plural] go-by-vehicle
Where are you going?

Что тебе нравится?
shtaw tyib*ye* nr*a*vitsa
what to-you³-[informal] pleases-self
What do you like?

Как вас зовут?
kak vas zav*oo*t
how you⁴-[formal/plural] [they]-call
What's your name?

Кто это?
ktaw *e*ta
who that
Who's that?

Что это?
shtaw *e*ta
what that
What's that?

Кто там?
ktaw tam
who there
Who's there?

Что там?
shtaw tam
what there
What's there? /
What's that over there?

Что случилось?
shtaw sloochilas^{yi}
what happened-self
What happened?

When you see someone you know whom you haven't seen for a long time, you can use the expression below to express your delight or surprise:

Кого я вижу!
kava<u>w</u> ya vi<u>zh</u>oo
whom I see
Look who's here!

NUMBERS

Cardinal Numbers

The numbers 1 and 2 and all numbers ending in 1 or 2 (21, 22, 31, 32, etc. except 11 and 12) agree in gender (m., f. or n.) with the noun they qualify. All other numbers are invariable.

0	ноль	*nawl^{yi}*
1	один, одна, одно (m./f./n.)	*adin / adna / adnaw*
2	два (m./n.), две (f.)	*dva / dvye*
3	три	*tri*
4	четыре	*chyiteeryi*
5	пять	*pyat^s*
6	шесть	*shest^s*
7	семь	*syem^{yi}*
8	восемь	*vawsyim^{yi}*
9	девять	*dyevyit^s*
10	десять	*dyesyit^s*

11	одиннадцать	*adin<u>a</u>tsat^s*
12	двенадцать	*dvyin<u>a</u>tsat^s*
13	тринадцать	*trin<u>a</u>tsat^s*
14	четырнадцать	*chyit<u>ee</u>rnatsat^s*
15	пятнадцать	*pyitn<u>a</u>tsat^s*
16	шестнадцать	*shyisn<u>a</u>tsat^s*
17	семнадцать	*syimn<u>a</u>tsat^s*
18	восемнадцать	*vasyimn<u>a</u>tsat^s*
19	девятнадцать	*dyivyitn<u>a</u>tsat^s*

Note that the numbers from 11 to 19 all end in **-надцать** *natsat^s*.

10	десять	*dy<u>e</u>syit^s*
20	двадцать	*dv<u>a</u>tsat^s*
30	тридцать	*tr<u>i</u>tsat^s*
40	сорок	*s<u>aw</u>rak*
50	пятьдесят	*pyit'dyis<u>ya</u>t*
60	шестьдесят	*shyist'dyis<u>ya</u>t*
70	семьдесят	*sy<u>e</u>m'dyisyit*
80	восемьдесят	*v<u>aw</u>syim'dyisyit*
90	девяносто	*dyivyin<u>aw</u>sta*
100	сто	*st<u>aw</u>*
200	двести	*dv<u>ye</u>sti*
300	триста	*tr<u>i</u>sta*
400	четыреста	*chyit<u>ee</u>ryista*
500	пятьсот	*pyit's<u>aw</u>t*
1,000	тысяча	*t<u>ee</u>syicha*
10,000	десять тысяч	*dy<u>e</u>syit' t<u>ee</u>syich*
100,000	сто тысяч	*st<u>aw</u> t<u>ee</u>syich*
1,000,000	один миллион	*ad<u>i</u>n mili<u>aw</u>n*

The letter **-ь** *yi/s* is usually only audible when a number is pronounced alone, or at the end of a sentence. In a sentence, it is not pronounced.

Numbers are formed in the same order as in English, i.e. thousands, hundreds, tens, units. Russian does not use "and" in numbers:

21	**двадцать один / двадцать одна / двадцать одно** *dvatsat' adin / dvatsat' adna / dvatsat' adnaw* twenty-one (m., f., n.)
22	**двадцать два / двадцать две** *dvatsat' dva / dvatsat' dvye* twenty-two (m., n./f.)
121	**сто двадцать один** *staw dvatsat' adin* one hundred and twenty-one (m.)
2333	**две тысячи триста тридцать три** *dvye teesyichi trista tritsat' tri* two thousand three hundred and thirty-three

Counting

When counting, Russians often say **раз** *ras, (one) time / once* instead of **один** *adin, one*.

Раз, два, три!
ras dva tri
once two three
One, two, three!

In Russian, the plural starts at... five! But when there is more than one of something, the noun that comes after the number must take the genitive case:

The number...	must be followed by...
1 (21, 31, 41, etc.)	Case 1 (nominative) singular
2, 3, 4 (22-24, 32-34, etc.)	Case 2 (genitive) singular
5-20 (25-30, 35-40, etc.)	Case 2 (genitive) plural

один рубль	**одна лодка**	**одно окно**
adin roobl[yi]	*adna lawtka*	*adnaw aknaw*
one-[m.] ruble	one-[f.] boat	one-[n.] window
one ruble	one boat	one window

два рубля	**две лодки**	**два окна**
dva rooblya	*dvye lawtki*	*dva akna*
two-[m.] ruble[2]	two-[f.] boat[2]	two-[n.] window[2]
two rubles	two boats	two windows

семнадцать рублей		**шесть лодок**
syimnatsat' rooblyey		*shyest' lawdak*
seventeen rubles[2]		six boats[2]
seventeen rubles		six boats

Ordinal Numbers

Ordinal numbers are used to denote the position of people or things in relation to each other, e.g. "the sixth taxi". Like adjectives, they agree in gender (m., f. or n.) and number (sg. or pl.):

1st	**первый / первая / первое** (m./f./n.)	*pyervweey / pyervaya / pyervaye*
2nd	**второй / вторая / второе** (m./f./n.)	*ftaroy / ftaraya / ftaroye*
3rd	**третий / третья / третье** (m./f./n.)	*tryetiy / tryet[s]ya / tryet[s]ye*
4th	**четвёртый / четвёртая / четвёртое** (m./f./n.)	*chyitvyawrteey / chyitvyawrtaya / chyitvyawrtaye*
5th	**пятый**	*pyateey*
6th	**шестой**	*shyistoy*
7th	**седьмой**	*syid[yi]moy*
8th	**восьмой**	*vas[yi]moy*
9th	**девятый**	*dyivyateey*
10th	**десятый**	*dyisyateey*

N.B. Ordinal numbers from 11th to 20th are formed by replacing the **-ть** t^s ending with **-тый** *teey*:

11th	одиннадцатый	*adinatsateey*
12th	двенадцатый	*dvyinatsateey*
20th	двадцатый	*dvatsateey*

30th	тридцатый	*tritsateey*
40th	сороковой	*sarakavoy*
50th	пятидесятый	*pyitidyisyateey*
60th	шестидесятый	*shyistidyisyateey*
70th	семидесятый	*syimidyisyateey*
80th	восьмидесятый	*vas^{y}midyisyateey*
90th	девяностый	*dyivyinawsteey*
100th	сотый	*sawteey*

As in English, only the last element of compound ordinal numbers (i.e. with more than one element) is in ordinal form:

двадцать первый
dvatsat^s pyervweey
twenty first
twenty-first

тридцать второй
tritsat^s ftaroy
thirty second
thirty-second

AGE

To express age, Russians count in years for the first five years, then in "summers" after that:

- 1 (and 21, 31, 41, etc. see above): **год** *gawt*, year;
- 2, 3 and 4 (and 22-24, 32-34, 42-44, etc.): **года** *gawda* (genitive sg. of **год** *gawt*), years;
- 5 to 20 (then 25-30, 35-40, etc.): **лет** *lyet*, summers.

To express "how old" someone is, the personal pronoun is in the dative case.

Сколько тебе/вам лет?
skawl[y]ka tyibye/vam lyet
how-many to-you-[informal]³/you-[formal/plural]³ summers²
How old are you?

Мне двадцать один год.
mnye dvatsat' adin gawt
to-me³ twenty one year
I'm 21.

Мне тридцать два года.
mnye tritsat' dva gawda
to-me³ thirty two of-year²
I'm 32.

Ему пятьдесят лет.
yimoo pyitdyisyat lyet
to-him³ fifty of-summers²
He's 50.

МНЕ ДВАДЦАТЬ ОДИН ГОД.
(I'm twenty-one.)

WEIGHTS AND MEASURES

Units of measurement decline. They take the case that is governed by the preceding number (see **Numbers**). The noun that comes after the unit of measurement takes the genitive (Case 2).

один литр воды *ad<u>i</u>n litr vad<u>ee</u>* one liter of-water[2] a liter of water	**три литра воды** *tri l<u>i</u>tra vad<u>ee</u>* three of-liter[2] of-water[2] three liters of water

много	*mn<u>a</u>wga*	a lot, many
немало	*ny<u>i</u>mala*	
мало	*m<u>a</u>la*	few, not many
сколько	*sk<u>a</u>wl^yika*	how many
немного	*nyimn<u>a</u>wga*	some, a few
несколько	*ny<u>e</u>skalk^yika*	

All nouns that come after one of the above indefinite adverbs of quantity take the genitive (Case 2) plural:

несколько друзей *ny<u>e</u>skal^yika drooz<u>ye</u>y* some of-friends[2] some friends	**много книг** *mn<u>a</u>wga knik* a-lot of-books[2] a lot of books

сто граммов	*staw gr<u>a</u>mmaf*	100 grams (100 grams[2])
один килограмм	*ad<u>i</u>n kilagr<u>a</u>m*	1 kilogram
полкило	*polkil<u>a</u>w*	½ kilogram
один литр	*ad<u>i</u>n litr*	1 liter
два литра	*dva l<u>i</u>tra*	2 liters (2 liter[2])
пол-литра	*pal-l<u>i</u>tra*	½ liter (½-liter[2])
один метр	*ad<u>i</u>n myetr*	1 meter

сто метров	*staw myetraf*	100 meters (100 meters²)
один километр	*adin kilamyetr*	1 kilometer
десять километров	*dyesyat' kilamyetraf*	10 kilometers (10 kilometers²)

одна коробка	*adna karawpka*	a box
половина	*palavina*	half
одна банка	*adna banka*	a jar/can
одна пара	*adna para*	a pair
один кулёк	*adin koolyawk*	a paper bag / packet (e.g. of candy)
одна штука	*adna shtooka*	a piece / one item

CONVERSATION

MINI GUIDE TO RUSSIAN ETIQUETTE

Modesty, patience and hospitality are the traits that best define the Russian character. In this vast country, you will often encounter a humanity and generosity that you don't see as often in the West.
Since the transition to a market economy, the large cities have become very money-oriented and consumeristic. In tourist areas, you will often encounter people eager to "do business" with you.
Wander off the beaten track and explore the back streets, stroll through parks, ride on public transport, or attend an Orthodox mass. That's where you'll find the real Russian soul!

If you wish to attend a religious service in a Russian Orthodox church, be sure to dress decently, especially in summer. No shorts, for men or women! Women are expected to cover their heads. Apart from that, there are no strict dress codes in Russia, although, as a general rule, people tend to dress more formally than in the West.

You will see many beggars in Russia, especially outside churches. They are often elderly, disabled or unemployed. They do not qualify for welfare benefits. They are destitute and totally dependent on the generosity of their fellow citizens, who are fairly compassionate as a general rule. Begging is certainly not a solution, but unlike us, Russians do not cross the street to avoid a beggar, and often give a few coins. Most of the people you see begging in Russia are genuinely in need, and a few rubles (hardly a sacrifice for us) can buy them a hot meal.

ВОСЕМЬДЕСЯТ СЕМЬ

Sign Language

Gestures and hand signals mean different things in different cultures.
To hail a taxi or hitch a ride (e.g. to the nearest garage if your car breaks down), you'll first have to wait for a car, which is not so common on small roads, then signal as follows:

- Hold your arm outstretched with your palm facing the road. A closed fist with a thumb up means "Everything's fine!" in Russia. If you try to flag down a vehicle like this, Russians will drive by, assuming you don't need anything.

- Tapping on your throat with thumb and forefinger joined means "Let's have a drink" or "He's drunk!".

TIME

Key Words

сегодня	syiv<u>aw</u>dnya	today
вчера	fch<u>yi</u>ra	yesterday
завтра	z<u>a</u>ftra	tomorrow
послезавтра	pawsly<u>e</u>z<u>a</u>ftra	the day after tomorrow
утро	<u>oo</u>tra	morning
день (m.)	dyen^{yi}	day
вечер	v<u>ye</u>chyir	evening
ночь (f.)	nawch'	night
утром	<u>oo</u>tram	in the morning
в полдень	f-p<u>aw</u>ldyen^{yi}	at midday
после обеда	p<u>aw</u>slye ab<u>ye</u>da	in the afternoon
днём	dnyawm	during the day
вечером	v<u>ye</u>chyiram	in the evening
ночью	n<u>aw</u>ch^{yi}yoo	at night
ежедневно	yezhyidn<u>ye</u>vna	every day

сегодня утром	syiv<u>aw</u>dnya <u>oo</u>tram	this morning
вчера вечером	fchir<u>a</u> vy<u>e</u>chyiram	yesterday evening
завтра утром	z<u>a</u>ftra <u>oo</u>tram	tomorrow morning
завтра вечером	z<u>a</u>ftra vy<u>e</u>chyiram	tomorrow evening
рано	r<u>a</u>na	early
поздно	p<u>aw</u>zna	late
раньше	r<u>a</u>n^{yi}she	earlier
позже	p<u>aw</u>zhzhe	later
теперь	tyipy<u>e</u>r^{yi}	now
никогда	nikagd<u>a</u>	never
иногда	inagd<u>a</u>	sometimes
часто	ch<u>a</u>sta	often
недавно	nyid<u>a</u>vna	not long ago
скоро	sk<u>aw</u>ra	soon
тому назад	tam<u>oo</u> naz<u>a</u>t	ago
после	p<u>aw</u>slye	after

Три дня (тому) назад.
tri dnya (tam<u>oo</u>) naz<u>a</u>t
three of-day[2] (to-this) behind
Three days ago.

Три дня.
tri dnya
three of-day[2]
For three days.

Через день/неделю/год.
ch<u>y</u>iryis dyen^{yi}/nyidy<u>e</u>lyoo/gawt
through day[4]/week[4]/year[4]
In a day / a week / a year.

Telling the Time

час	chas	hour
минута	min<u>oo</u>ta	minute
секунда	syik<u>oo</u>nda	second
по московскому времени	pa mask<u>aw</u>vskamoo vry<u>e</u>myini	Moscow time

восемьдесят девять 89

To ask the time, you say:

Который час?
kat<u>aw</u>reey chas
which hour
What time is it?

When saying what time it is, make sure the word **час** *chas*, *hour / o'clock* agrees with the number before it (see **Numbers**). Russian uses a 24-hour clock, e.g. **двадцать часов** *dv<u>a</u>tsat' chis<u>aw</u>f*, "twenty hours" = *8 p.m.*

ноль часов
nawl^{yi} chis<u>aw</u>f
zero hours[2]
midnight

один час
ad<u>i</u>n chas
one hour[1]
one o'clock

КОТОРЫЙ ЧАС?
(What time is it?)

| **два/три/четыре часа**
dva/tri/chit<u>ee</u>rye chis<u>a</u>
two/three/four of-hour[2] | two/three/four hours
(o'clock) |

пять/.../двадцать часов *pyat'/.../dvatsat' chisawf* five/.../twenty of-hours[2]	five/.../twenty hours (5 a.m. – 8 p.m.)
двадцать один час *dvatsat' adin chas* twenty one of-hour[2]	twenty-one hours (9 p.m.)
двадцать два/три/четыре часа *dvatsat' dva/tri/chiteerye chisa* twenty two/three/four of-hour[2]	twenty two/three/four hours (10 p.m./11 p.m./12 a.m.)

The way to say "a quarter past", "ten to", etc. is quite complicated. We suggest you take the easy way and express time as "X hours, Y minutes".

Like **час** *chas*, hour, **минута** *minoota*, minute declines: **две/три/четыре минуты** *dvye/tri/chiteerye minootee*, two/three/four minutes (genitive singular), **пять/шесть/семь/восемь/девять/десять минут** *pyat'/shest'/syem[yi]/vawsim[yi]/dyevyit'/dyesyit' minoot*, five/six/seven/eight/nine/ten minutes (genitive plural). As in English, the word "minute" can be left out.

в час
f-chas
at hour
at one o'clock / at 1 a.m./p.m.

в три часа пятнадцать минут
f-tri chisa pyitnatsat' minoot
at three of-hour[2] fifteen of-minutes[2]
at 3.15 a.m./p.m.

в десять часов сорок пять минут
v-dyesyit' chisawf sawrak pyat' minoot
at ten of-hours[2] forty five of-minutes[2]
at 10.45 a.m./p.m.

в двадцать два часа две минуты
v-dvatsat' dva chisa dvye minootee
at twenty two of-hour² two of-minute²
at 10.02 p.m.

The earth has 24 time zones. Russia spans 11 of them. When the residents of Saint Petersburg are having dinner, people in the far east of Russia are eating breakfast! The town of **Анадырь** *anadeer*ʸⁱ, *Anadyr*, is on the same meridian as New Zealand and Fiji.

Moscow is three hours ahead of London and eight hours ahead of Washington D.C.

Seasons

весна	*vyisna*	spring
лето	*lyeta*	summer
осень	*awsyin*ʸⁱ	autumn/fall
зима	*zima*	winter

Holidays

праздник	*praznik*	holiday, special occasion
семейный праздник	*syimyeyneey praznik*	family reunion
пасха	*paskha*	Easter
троица	*trawitsa*	Pentecost
рождество	*razhdyistvaw*	Christmas

The official holidays in Russia are:

первое января	*pyervaye yinvarya*	January 1
новый год	*nawvweey gawt*	New Year*
седьмое января	*syid*ʸⁱ*moye yinvarya*	January 7 (Russian Orthodox Christmas)

двадцать третье февраля	dvatsat' tretsye fyivralya	February 23 (Protector of the Fatherland Day also known as Army Day)
восьмое марта	vasyimoye marta	March 8 (International Women's Day)
первое мая	pyervaye maya	May 1 (Labor Day)
девятое мая	dyivyataye maya	May 9 (WWII Victory Day)
двенадцатое июня	dvyinatsataye iyoonya	June 12 (Russia Day), commemorating Russia's independence from the USSR in 1991
четвёртое ноября	chyitvyawrtaye nayibrya	November 4 (Day of National Unity)
двенадцатое декабря	dvyinatsataye dyikabrya	December 12 (Constitution Day)

* In Soviet times, New Year's Eve replaced the religious holiday of Christmas. New Year's Eve is still the biggest secular holiday, celebrated with Santa Claus, fir trees and gift giving, as well as fireworks and concerts.

Days of the Week

понедельник	panyidyelyinik	Monday
вторник	vtawrnik	Tuesday
среда	sryida	Wednesday

девяносто три

четверг	chyitv_yerk_	Thursday
пятница	p_ya_tnitsa	Friday
суббота	soob_aw_ta	Saturday
воскресенье	vaskryis_ye_nye	Sunday

Months

январь	yinv_ar_[yi]	January
февраль	fyivr_al_[yi]	February
март	mart	March
апрель	apr_yel_[yi]	April
май	may (pronounced like English "my")	May
июнь	i_yoon_[yi]	June
июль	i_yool_[yi]	July
август	_av_goost	August
сентябрь	syinty_a_br[yi]	September
октябрь	akt_ya_br[yi]	October
ноябрь	nay_a_br[yi]	November
декабрь	dyik_a_br[yi]	December

All the months are masculine.

Dates

Какое сегодня число?
kak_aw_ye syiv_aw_dnya chisl_aw_
which today date
What is the date today?

To say the date, use a neuter ordinal number followed by the month in the genitive case (Case 2) singular:

Сегодня четвёртое апреля.
syiv_aw_dnya chyitv_yaw_rtaye apr_ye_lya
today fourth-[n.] of-April[2]
Today is the fourth of April.

Второе марта.
ftar_aw_ye m_a_rta
second-[n.] of-March[2]
The second of March.

NAMES AND TERMS OF ADDRESS

All Russians have a first name, a middle name, and a surname (family name). The middle name, or "patronymic", is derived from their father's first name. The endings of the patronymic and surname change depending on the person's gender. Only the surname is passed on from generation to generation.

имя	отчество	фамилия
imya	*awtchyistva*	*familiya*
first name	patronymic	surname
Виктор	**Иванович**	**Андропов**
viktar	*ivanavich*	*andrawpaf*
Тамара	**Ивановна**	**Андропова**
tamara	*ivanavna*	*andrawpava*

In the example above, the names Victor Ivanovich Andropov and Tamara Ivanovna Andropova indicate that Victor and Tamara's father's name was Ivan.

Anyone who has read Russian literature will know that Russians are also very fond of diminutives (nicknames). Don't be surprised by the many different names one person is called. These are just affectionate variations of the same name. Diminutives are used for both children and adults:

Александр	**Саша / Шура**
alyiksandr	*sasha / shoora*
Владимир	**Володя / Вова**
vladimir	*valawdya / vawva*
Людмила	**Люда / Люся / Мила**
lyoodmila	*lyooda / lyoosya / mila*

The polite way to address one or several people is **вы** *vwee*, *you*. It is used in the same way as *vous* in French. It takes some getting used to for English speakers.

девяносто пять

Где вы живёте
gdye vwee zheevyawtye
where you-[formal/plural] live
Where do you live?

If you aren't sure whether to use the **ты** *tee*, *(informal) you* or **вы** *vwee*, *(formal) you* form with someone, it is always best to use **вы** *vwee*.

Может быть, мы перейдём на ты?
mawzhet bweet⁵ mwee pyiryiydyawm na tee
may be we go-across to you-[informal]
Perhaps we could use informal you with each other?

To address someone, there is no direct equivalent of "Sir" or "Madam". There are different expressions, depending on the context. When you don't know the person's name, use the forms of address on the next page.

МОЖЕТ БЫТЬ, МЫ ПЕРЕЙДЁМ НА ТЫ?
(Perhaps we could use informal you with each other?)

Some government institutions (e.g. courthouses, police stations), use the highly official form, followed by the person's surname:

гражданин	grazhdan*in*	citizen (m.)
гражданка	grazhd*a*nka	citizen (f.)
гражданин Иванов	grazhdan*in* ivan*aw*f	Citizen Ivanov

Russians will usually use the (very) polite form to address someone formally. You can use it too:

господин	gaspad*in*	Mr.
госпожа	gaspazh*a*	Miss/Mrs./Ms.
госпожа Джонс	gaspazh*a* dzhawns	Miss/Mrs./Ms. Jones

To call a waiter/waitress in a cafe or restaurant, say:

Девушка!	d*ye*vooshka	Miss!
Официант!	afits*ant*	Waiter!

In their day-to-day dealings (with colleagues, neighbors, etc.), Russians call each other by their first name + patronymic. This is a polite form of address and is used with **вы** vwee, *(formal) you*:

Здравствуйте, Тамара Ивановна!
zdr*a*stvooytye tam*a*ra iv*a*navna
Hello, Tamara Ivanovna!

The form **товарищ** tav*a*rishch, *comrade*, very common before the collapse of the Soviet Union, is now only used jokingly and should therefore be avoided.

SAYING HELLO

Доброе утро!
d*aw*braye *oo*tra
Good morning!

Добрый день!
d*aw*breey dyen[yi]
Good day!
("hello" during the day)

Добрый вечер!
dawbreey vyechyir
Good evening!

You can also say the following at any time of the day:

Здравствуй!
zdrastvooy
be-healthy-[informal]
Hello!

Здравствуйте!
zdrastvooytye
be-healthy-[formal/plural]
Hello!

Among young people and with friends, you're more likely to hear:

Привет!
privyet
greetings
Hi!

Как дела?
kak dyila
how things
How are you? / How's it going?

Other common expressions:

Я рад/рада видеть тебя/вас!
ya rat/rada vidyit⁵ tyibya/vas
I glad-[m./f.] to-see you-[informal / formal/plural]
I'm glad to see you!

Добро пожаловать!
dabraw pazhalavat⁵
good to-come-to-see
Welcome!

Как (вы) поживаете?
kak (vwee) pazheevayite
how (you)-[formal/plural] live
How are you?

Спасибо, хорошо!
spasiba kharashaw
thank-you well
Well, thank you!

К сожалению, плохо.
k-sazhilyeniyoo plawkha
with regret badly
Unfortunately, bad.

Что случилось?
shtaw sloochilas[yi]
what happened-self
What happened?

SAYING GOODBYE

До свидания!
da svidaniya
until seeing-again
Goodbye!

До завтра!
da zaftra
until tomorrow
See you tomorrow!

... to friends and close family:

До скорого!
da skawrava
until of-soon
See you soon!

Пока!
paka
Bye!

In general:

Всего хорошего!
fsyivaw kharawsheeva
of-all of-good
All the best! / Goodbye!

Доброй ночи!
dawbray nawchi
Good night!

Увидимся ли мы ещё?
oovidimsya li mwee yishchyaw
[we]-see-self [question-word] we again
Will we see each other again?

Передайте привет вашей жене / вашему мужу!
pyiryidaytye privyet vashey zhenye / vashemoo moozhoo
pass-on greetings your[3] wife[3] / your[3] husband[3]
Say hello to your wife / to your husband [from me]!

девяносто девять

Мне пора!
mnye par*a*
for-me³ time
It's time for me (to go)!

Я должен/должна идти.
ya d*a*wlzhen/dalzhn*a* itti
I must-[m./f.] to-go
I have to go.

Я вернусь снова.
ya vyirn*oo*s^(yi) sn*a*wva
I will-return-[perf.] again
I'll be back.

Мы обязательно придём ещё раз.
mwee abyizatyil^(yi)na pridy*a*wm yishch*y*aw ras
we definitely will-come again time
We'll definitely come again.

Счастливого пути!
shchistl*i*vava p*oo*ti
happy path²
Bon voyage! /
Have a safe trip!

Пишите, пожалуйста!
pish*ee*tye pazh*a*lsta
write-[!] please
Please write (to us)!

Ты милый человек / милая женщина!
tee m*i*leey chyilav*ye*k / m*i*laya zh*e*nshchina
you-[informal] sweet-[m.] man / sweet-[f.] woman
You're very nice.

ASKING, THANKING, BEING POLITE

Asking for Something

У меня большая просьба!
oo myiny*a* bal^(yi)sh*a*ya pr*a*wz^(yi)ba
in-the-possession of-me² big request
I'd like to ask something!

Дайте мне, пожалуйста... !
daytye mnye pazhalsta
give-[!] to-me³ please
Could you please give me...

Пожалуйста *pazhalsta* means *please* but also *you're welcome* after someone says thank you.

Можете ли вы мне/нам помочь?
mawzhetye li vwee mnye/nam pamawch'
can [question-word] you-[formal/plural] to-me³/to-us³ to-help
Can you help me/us?

You can begin a request with "Do you permit me to...?". That might sound extremely formal in English, but it is extremely common in Russian and a courteous way to address people you don't know. See the chapter on imperatives, which contains several similar expressions.

If you were to learn just one expression, the easiest and most useful is: **можно** *mawzhna*, *May I/we?*, *Is... allowed?*

Разрешите...?
razryisheetye
permit-[!]
Would you let me...? /
Do you mind if I...?

Могу ли я...?
magoo-li ya
can [question-word] I
May I...?

Можно курить?
mawzhna koorit's
is-it-allowed to-smoke
Is smoking permitted? / Can you smoke here?

Разрешите войти?
razryisheetye vayti
permit-[!] to-enter
May I / May we come in?

сто один

Можно фотографировать?
mawzhna fatagrafiravatʲ
is-it-allowed to-take-photographs
Is taking photographs permitted? / Can you take photos here?

Saying Thank You

Большое спасибо!
balʲyishoye spasiba
big thanks
Thank you very much!

Спасибо!
spasiba
thanks
Thank you!

Вы очень добры!
vwee awchyinʲyi dabree
you-[formal/plural] very good-[pl.]
That's very kind of you!

Я благодарю вас от всего сердца!
ya blagadaryoo vas at fsyivaw² syertsa
I thank you-[formal/plural] from whole² heart²
I thank you from the bottom of my heart!

(Пожалуйста) не за что!
(pazhalsta) nye-za-shtaw
(please) not for that
Not at all! / It was nothing!

Сердечное спасибо!
syirdyechnaye spasiba
heartfelt thanks
Heartfelt thanks!

Спасибо, вам тоже!
spasiba vam tawzhe
thanks to-you³-[formal/plural] too
Thank you, you too!

Wishing

(Я тебя/вас) поздравляю с днём рождения!
(ya tyibya/vas) pazdravlyayoo z-dyawm razhdyeniya
(I you-[informal]/you-[formal/plural]) congratulate with day⁵ of-birth²
Happy birthday!

102 сто два

(Я) желаю тебе/вам...!
(ya) zhelayoo tyibye/vam
(I) wish to-you[3]-[informal]/you[3]-[formal/plural]
I wish you...!

... счастья!	shchastya	of-happiness[2]	... happiness/luck!
... здоровья!	zdarawvya	of-health[2]	... health (good ~!)
... успехов!	oospyekhaf	of-successes[2]	... success!

Всего хорошего!
fsyivaw kharawsheeva
of-all[2] of-good[2]
All the best! / Goodbye!

Желаю...	zhelayoo	I-wish	I wish you...
... удачи!	oodachi	success	... success!
... поправиться!	papravitsa	to-correct-self	... a quick recovery!

Много счастья!
mnawga shchast'ya
much luck[2]
Good luck!

Сердечные поздравления!
syirdyechneeye pazdravlyeniya
heartfelt congratulations
Best wishes!

За здоровье!
za-darawv'ye
for health[4]
Cheers!

С Новым годом!
s-nawveem gawdam
with new[5] year[5]
Happy New Year!

С праздником!
s-praznikam
with holiday[5]
Happy holiday! (for any holiday or feast day)

Будьте здоровы!
boot'tye zdarawvwee
be-[!] healthy-[pl.]
Bless you! (after someone sneezes)

сто три 103

(Я тебе/вам) желаю счастливого нового года!
(ya tyibye/vam) zhelayoo shchistlivaya nawvava gawda
(I to-you-[informal][3]/to-you-[formal/plural][3]) wish happy[2] new[2] year[2]
I wish you a happy new year!

Большое спасибо за поздравления!
bal[yi]shoye spasiba za pazdravlyeniya
big thanks for congratulations[4]
Thank you very much for your kind wishes!

Apologizing, Expressing Regret

Извините!
izvinitye
excuse
Sorry! / Excuse me!

Простите!
prastitye
forgive
Sorry! / Forgive me!

Это ужасно!
eta oozhasna
that awful
That's awful!

Мне очень жаль!
mnye awchyin[yi] zhal[yi]
me[3] very pity
I'm so sorry!

Как жаль!
kak zhal[yi]
how pity
What a pity! /
That's a shame!

Очень жаль!
awchyin[yi] zhal[yi]
very pity
That's such a pity! /
That's a real shame!

К сожалению, я не могу остаться/прийти!
k-sazhilyeniyoo ya nyi magoo astatsa/priyti
to regret[3] I not can to-stay/to-come
Unfortunately, I can't stay/come!

ACCEPTING AND REFUSING

Accepting and Complimenting

Всё в порядке!	*fsyaw f-paryatkye*	Everything's fine! (all in order)

Хорошо!	kharashaw	Good!
Я знаю. / Мы знаем.	ya znayoo / mwee znayim	I know. / We know.
Разумеется!	razoomyeyitsa	It goes without saying! / Of course!
Конечно!	kanyeshna	Of course!
Правильно!	pravil[yi]na	Right!
(Это) красиво!	(eta) krasiva	That's beautiful!
(Это) отлично!	(eta) atlichna	That's excellent!
(Это) верно!	(eta) vyerna	That's true!
(Это) прекрасно!	(eta) prikrasna	That's wonderful!
С (большим) удовольствием	s (bal[yi]sheem) oodavawl[yi]stviyem	With (great) pleasure!
Да!	da	Yes!

Я/Ты прав/права!
ya/tee praf/prava
I/you-[informal] right-[m./f.]
I'm/You're right!

Мы/Вы правы!
mwee/vwee pravwee
we/you-[formal/plural] right-[m./f.]
We're/You're right!

Это мне (очень) нравится!
eta mnye (awchyin[yi]) nravitsa
that to-me[3] (very) likes-self
I (really) like that!

If you are not quite as enthusiastic:

Пойдёт!	poydyawt	That's fine/good enough!
Возможно!	vazmawzhna	Perhaps!
Вероятно!	vyirayatna	Probably!
Я не знаю.	ya nyi znayoo	I don't know.

Refusing and Disagreeing

Нет!	nyet	No!
Нет, спасибо!	nyet spasiba	No, thank you!

сто пять

Конечно, нет!	kan**ye**shna nyet	Of course not!
Никогда!	nikag**da**	Never!
Ни в коем случае!	ni-f-**ka**wyem sl**oo**chiye	No way!
Ниправильно!	nipr**a**vil[yi]na	Wrong!
Этого не было!	**e**tava n**ye**-bweela	That never happened!
Напротив!	napr**aw**tif	On the contrary!

Ты не прав/права.
tee nyi praf/pr**a**va
you-[informal] not right-[m./f.]
You're wrong.

Это не возможно.
eta nyi vazm**aw**zhna
that not possible
That's impossible.

Это мне не нравится.
eta mnye nyi nr**a**vitsa
that to-me³ not likes-self
I don't like that.

У меня нет желания.
oo myin**ya** nyet zhel**a**niya
in-the-possession of-me² no wish²
I don't feel like it.

Вы ошибаетесь!
vwee asheeb**a**yityes[yi]
you-[formal/plural] mistake-self
You're mistaken!

Я хочу пожаловаться на...
ya khach**oo** pazh**a**lavatsa na
I want to-complain-self on...⁴
I wish to complain about...

INTRODUCTIONS

Я рад/рада с вами познакомиться.
ya rat/r**a**da s-v**a**mi paznak**aw**mitsa
I glad-[m./f.] with you⁵-[formal/plural] to-acquaint-self
Pleased to meet you.

Разрешите представиться: господин Гордон.
razryish**ee**tye pryitst**a**vitsa gasp**a**din g**o**rdan
permit-[!]-[formal/plural] to-present-self Mr. Gordon
Allow me to introduce myself: I am Mr. Gordon.

Очень приятно.
awchyin^yi priyatna
very pleasant
Nice to meet you.

Мне тоже.
mnye tawzhe
for-me³ too
You too. / Likewise.

Не могли бы Вы познакомить меня с господином Андроповым?
nyi magli bwee vwee paznak<u>aw</u>mit⁵ myinya z-gaspadinam andr<u>aw</u>pavweem
not could [conditional-particle] you-[formal/plural] to-acquaint me² with Mr.⁵ Andropov⁵
Could you introduce me to Mr. Andropov?

Разрешите представиться?
razryish<u>ee</u>tye pryitst<u>a</u>vitsa
permit-[!]-[formal/plural] to-present-self
Allow me to introduce myself.

Моя фамилия Робертс.
maya familiya rawbyirts
my surname Roberts
My (sur)name is Roberts.

Это моя жена / мой муж.
eta maya zhena / moy moosh
this my wife / my husband
This is my wife / my husband.

Striking Up a Conversation

Как тебя/вас зовут?
kak tyibya/vas zavoot
how you²-[informal]/you²-[formal/plural] they-call
What's your name?

Меня зовут Мария.
myinya zavoot mariya
me² they-call Maria
My name is Maria.

Откуда ты/вы?
atkooda tee/vwee
where-from you-[informal]/you-[formal/plural]
Where are you from?

ЭТО МОЯ ЖЕНА.
(This is my wife.)

ЭТО МОЙ МУЖ.
(This is my husband.)

Я/Мы из Америки/Канады/Англии/Австралии.
ya/mwee iz-amyeriki/kanadee/anglii/afstralii
I/we from America[2]/Canada[2]/England[2]/Australia[2]
I'm/We're from America/Canada/England/Australia.

Из какого города вы приехали?
is-kakawva gawrada vwee priyekhali
from which[2] city[2] you-[formal/plural] come
Which city do you come from?

Я/Мы из...
ya/mwee iz
I/we from...[2]
I'm/We're from...

Since there's a good chance the people you speak to won't have heard of your home town, it makes it slightly clearer if you use the word **города** gawrada, *city*, before the name of your town.

N.B. The name of the town or city must also be in the genitive case.

Я из (города) Нью-Йорка/Ванкувера/Лондона/Сиднея.
ya iz (gawrada) nyoo-yawrka/vankoovyira/lawndana/sidnyeya
I from (city[2]) New York[2]/Vancouver[2]/London[2]/Sydney[2]
I'm from (the city of) New York, Vancouver, London, Sydney.

Где ты остановился/остановилась?
gdye tee astanavilsya/astanavilas[yi]
where you-[informal] stopped-self-[m./f.]
Where are you staying?

Где вы остановились?
gdye vwee astanavilis[yi]
where you-[formal/plural] stopped-self
Where are you staying?

Я остановился/остановилась / Мы остановились в гостинице.
ya astanavilsya/astanavilas[yi] / mwee astanavilis[yi] v-gastinitse
I stopped-self-[m./f.] / we stopped-self at hotel
I am staying / We are staying at a hotel.

Что ты здесь делаешь?
shtaw tee zdyes[yi] dyelayish'
what you-[informal] here do
What are you doing here?

Что вы здесь делаете?
shtaw vwee zdyes[yi] dyelayitye
what you-[formal/plural] here do
What are you doing here?

Я турист/туристка.
ya toorist/tooristka
I tourist-[m./f.]
I'm a tourist.

Я здесь работаю.
ya zdyes[yi] rabawtayoo
I here work
I work here.

Я приехал/приехала по делам.
ya priyekhal/priyekhala pa dyilam
I came-[m./f.] for things[3]
I came on business.

Вы живёте одни?
vwee zheevyawtye adni
you-[formal] live alone-[pl.]
Do you live alone?

Ты живёшь один/одна?
tee zheevyawsh' adin/adna
you-[informal] live alone-[m./f]
Do you live alone?

Да, я живу один/одна.
da ya zheevoo adin/adna
yes I live alone-[m./f.]
Yes, I live alone.

Нет, я женат/замужем.
nyet ya zhenat/zamoozhem
no I married-[male speaker]/married-[female speaker]
No, I'm married.

У вас есть дети?
oo vas yest⁵ dyeti
in-the-possession of-you[2]-[formal/plural] there-is children
Do you have children?

У нас нет детей.
oo nas nyet dyityey
in-the-possession of-us[2] no children[2]
We don't have any children.

У вас есть братья или сёстры?
oo vas yest⁵ bratya ili syawstree
in-the-possession of-you[2]-[formal/plural] there-is brothers or sisters
Do you have any brothers or sisters?

У меня есть брат.
oo myinya yest⁵ brat
in-the-possession of-me[2] there-is brother
I have a brother.

Кем ты работаешь / вы работаете?
kyem tee rabawtayish' / vwee rabawtayitye
as-who[2] you-[informal] work / you-[formal/plural] work
What kind of work do you do?

Я (по профессии)...
ya (pa prafyesii)
I (by profession[3])
I'm a...

бизнесмен, предприниматель	*biznesmyen, pryitprinimatel[yi]*	businessman, entrepreneur
ремесленник	*ryimyeslyinnik*	craftsman
врач	*vrach*	doctor
служащий / служащая (m./f.)	*sloozhashchiy / sloozashchaya*	employee, office worker
инженер	*inzhenyer*	engineer
фермер	*fyermyir*	farmer
домохозяйка	*damakhazyayka*	homemaker
журналист / журналистка (m./f.)	*zhoornalist / zhoornalistka*	journalist
коммерсант	*kamyirsant*	merchant
пенсионер / пенсионерка (m./f.)	*pyinsianyer / pyinsianyerka*	pensioner
ученик / ученица (m./f.)	*oochyinik / oochyinitsa*	school student, apprentice
частник	*chastnik*	self-employed
студент / студентка (m./f.)	*stoodyent / stoodyentka*	student
учитель / учительница (m./f.)	*oochityil[yi] / oochityil[yi]nitsa*	teacher
безработный / безработная (m./f.)	*byizrabawtneey / byizrabawtnaya*	unemployed
рабочий / рабочая (m./f.)	*rabawchiy / rabawchaya*	worker (manual ~)

сто одиннадцать

Вам нравится в Москве?
vam nravitsa v-maskvye
to-you[3]-[formal/plural] it-pleases-self in Moscow[6]
Do you like being in Moscow?

Да, мне очень нравится.
da mnye awchyin[yi] nravitsa
yes to-me[3] very it-pleases-self
Yes, very much.

INVITATIONS

Я приглашаю вас!
ya priglashayoo vas
I invite you[4]-[formal/plural]
You're my guest! (let me pay for the drinks/meal, etc.)

Будьте нашим гостем!
boot[e]tye nasheem gawstyem
be-[!]-[formal/plural] our[5] guest[5]
Be our guest!

Приходите к нам домой завтра вечером!
prikhaditye k-nam damoy zaftra vyechyiram
come-[!]-[formal/plural] to us[3] home tomorrow evening
Come over tomorrow night!

Что вы делаете сегодня вечером?
shtaw vwee dyelayitye syivawdnya vyechyiram
what you-[formal/plural] do today evening
What are you doing tonight?

Хотите пойти с нами?
khatitye payti s-nami
want-[formal/plural] to-come with us[5]
Do you want to come with us?

С удовольствием!
s-oodavawl[yi]stviyim
with pleasure[5]
With pleasure!

Спасибо большое за приглашение!
spasiba bal[y]shoye za priglasheniye
thanks big for invitation[4]
Thank you very much for the invitation! / for inviting me!

Большое спасибо, но я не могу.
bal[y]shoye spasiba naw ya nyi magoo
big thanks but I not can
Thank you very much, but I can't come.

If Russian acquaintances invite you to their home, like everywhere they'll be delighted if you bring a small gift. If you do not know the kinds of things they like, you cannot go wrong with perfume (or cosmetics) or something typical from your country. In large cities, flowers or fresh produce from a market will also be appreciated.

In Russia, **подарки** *padarki*, *gifts*, are very important in day-to-day life. It is very common to give small gifts: to a nice chambermaid in a hotel, to helpful people in the street, to children who want to trade with you. Don't be surprised if Russians offer you gifts in return. So as not to be caught empty-handed, make sure to pack plenty of small gifts before you leave. It is not the value of the gift, but the thought that counts.

Мы принесли / Я принёс/принесла маленкий подарок.
mwee prinyisli / ya prinyaws/prinyisla malyinkiy padarak
we brought / I brought-[m./f.] small gift
We brought / I brought a small gift.

Вы голодны?
vwee galadnee
you-[formal/plural] hungry
Are you hungry?

Ты голодный/голодная?
tee galawdneey/galawdnaya
you-[informal] hungry-[m./f.]
Are you hungry?

сто тринадцать

Ты хочешь есть?
tee kh<u>aw</u>chyish' yest⁵
you-[informal] want to-eat
Are you hungry?

Ещё что-нибудь?
yishch<u>yaw</u> shtaw-nib<u>oo</u>t⁵
again anything
Something else?

Спасибо, охотно.
spas<u>i</u>ba akh<u>aw</u>tna
thanks willingly
Yes, please.

Нет, спасибо! Я действительно не могу больше!
nyet spas<u>i</u>ba! ya dyiystv<u>i</u>tyil^{yi}na nyi mag<u>oo</u> bawl^{yi}she
no thanks! I really not can more
No, thank you! I'm full!

Спасибо большое за хорошую еду / прекрасный вечер!
spas<u>i</u>ba bal^{yi}sh<u>aw</u>ye za khar<u>aw</u>shooyoo yid<u>oo</u> / prikr<u>a</u>sneey v<u>ye</u>chyir
thanks big⁴ for good⁴ food⁴ / lovely⁴ evening⁴
Thank you very much for a wonderful meal / a lovely evening!

Можно приготовить блюдо для вас?
m<u>aw</u>zhna prigat<u>aw</u>vit⁵ bly<u>oo</u>da dlya vas
it-is-possible to-prepare dish for you²-[formal/plural]
Can I/we prepare a [special] dish for you?

Вот фотографии из дома
vawt fatagr<u>a</u>fii iz d<u>aw</u>ma
here photographs from house²
Here are some photos from home.

Я дружу с...
ya droozh<u>oo</u> s
I befriend with...⁵
I'm friends with...

FAMILY

родители	*rad<u>i</u>tyili*	parents
родственники	*r<u>aw</u>tstvinniki*	relatives
отец, папа	*at<u>ye</u>ts, p<u>a</u>pa*	father, Dad

мать, мама	mat^s, mama	mother, Mom
муж	moosh	husband
жена	zhen<u>a</u>	wife
брат	brat	brother
сестра	syistr<u>a</u>	sister
зять	zyat^s	brother-in-law
золовка	zal<u>aw</u>fka	sister-in-law
ребёнок	ryib<u>yaw</u>nak	child
дети	d<u>ye</u>ti	children
сын	seen	son
дочь	dawch'	daughter
дядя	d<u>ya</u>dya	uncle
тётя	t<u>yaw</u>tya	aunt
племянник	plyim<u>ya</u>nnik	nephew
племянница	plyim<u>ya</u>nnitsa	niece
дедушка	d<u>ye</u>dooshka	grandfather
бабушка	b<u>a</u>booshka	grandmother
внук	vnook	grandson
внучка	vn<u>oo</u>chka	granddaughter

одинокий / одинокая	adin<u>aw</u>kiy / adin<u>aw</u>kaya	single (m./f.)
обручён / обручена	abroochy<u>aw</u>n / abroochyin<u>a</u>	engaged (m./f.)
женат / замужем	zhen<u>a</u>t / z<u>a</u>moozhem	married (m./f.)
разведён / разведена	razvyid<u>yaw</u>n / razvyidyin<u>a</u>	divorced (m./f.)
вдовец / вдова	vdavy<u>e</u>ts / vdav<u>a</u>	widower/widow

LOVE MATTERS...

СПИД	spit	AIDS
презерватив	pryizyirvat<u>i</u>f	condom

флиртовать	flirtavat[s]	flirt (to ~)
флирт	flirt	flirtation
целовать	tselavat[s]	kiss (to ~)
поцелуй	patseelooy	kiss
любовь	lyooba<u>w</u>f[yi]	love
защита	zashch<u>i</u>ta	protection

Ты мне нравишься.
tee mnye n<u>ra</u>vish'sya
you-[informal] to-me[3] please
I like you.

Я тебя люблю.
ya tyibya lyoobl<u>yo</u>o
I you[4]-[informal] love
I love you.

Хочешь спать со мной?
kha<u>w</u>chyish' spat[s] sa-mnoy
[you-informal]-want-to-sleep with me[5]
Do you want to sleep with me?

У меня есть презерватив.
oo myin<u>ya</u> yest[s] pryizyirvat<u>i</u>f
in-the-possession of-me[2] there-is condom
I have a condom.

Сегодня нет.
syiv<u>aw</u>dnya nyet
today no
Not today.

Оставь меня в покое!
asta<u>f</u>[yi] myin<u>ya</u> f-pak<u>o</u>ye
leave me[2] in peace[6]
Leave me alone!

TOILETS

Russians have two words for toilet – the more polite **туалет** *tooal<u>ye</u>t* and the more familiar **уборная** *oob<u>o</u>rnaya*. Stand-up toilets are fairly common. It's a good idea to carry toilet paper or paper tissues around with you.

| занято / свободно | z<u>a</u>nyita / svab<u>aw</u>dna | engaged / vacant |
| уборная | oob<u>o</u>rnaya | john |

Мужчина (**М** on toilet door)	*mooshchina*	Men
мужской туалет	*mooshskoy tooalyet*	men's toilet
туалет	*tooalyet*	toilet
туалетная бумага	*tooalyetnaya boomaga*	toilet paper
Женщина (**Ж** on toilet door)	*zhenshchina*	Women
женский туалет	*zhenskiy tooalyet*	women's toilet

Где здесь туалет?
gdye zdyes__yi__ tooalyet
where here toilet
Where is there a toilet near here?

У вас есть туалетная бумага?
oo vas yest__s__ tooalyetnaya boomaga
in-the-possession of-you-[formal/plural] there-is toilet paper
Do you have any toilet paper?

ГДЕ ЗДЕСЬ ТУАЛЕТ?
(Where are the toilets?)

INSULTS

It's fairly common to hear people – especially men – swearing in Russia. But, even if you're comfortable swearing at home, we advise against swearing in a foreign language.

As a foreigner, it is very hard to get a sense of when it is appropriate to swear in another language and how strong words sound. If you attempt to swear in Russian, there is a high chance you will sound either ridiculous or much more offensive than you intended. The words below are just so you understand them if you hear them:

Сволочь!	svawlach[yi]	Bastard! / Scum!
Чёрт! / К чёрту!	chyawrt / k-chyawrtoo	Damn it! (devil / to the devil)
Пошёл вон!	pashawl vawn	Fuck off! / Get out!
Дурак!	doorak	Idiot!
Ёлки-палки!	yawlki-palki	Shit! (fir-sticks)
(Ты) говно!	(tee) gavnaw	You piece of shit!

FINDING YOUR WAY AROUND TOWN

Don't be surprised if you can't find all the place names you see on your map. With recent political changes, many streets and landmarks have been renamed.
If you are on foot, pedestrian crossings are no guarantee of safety. Use underground crossings wherever possible.

Как мне пройти к...?
kak mnye prayti k
how to-me[3] to-go-through to...[3]
How do I get to...?

Можно пройти пешком?
mawzhna prayti pyishkawm
it-is-possible to-go-through on-foot
Is it within walking distance? / Can I/we walk there?

Далеко ещё до...?
dalyikaw yishchyaw da
far still to...[2]
How far are we from...?

Поезжайте на автобусе!
payizhzhaytye na aftawboosye
go-[!]-[plural/formal] on bus[6]
Take the bus!

Ещё...
yishchyaw
again
Another...

... пять минут
pyats minoot
... 5 minutes

... сто метров
staw myetraf
... 100 meters / block

... один километр
adin kilamyetr
... 1 kilometer

(On forming plurals after a number, see **The plural**).

Это улица...?
eta oolitsa
this street
Is this... Street?

Как называется эта улица?
kak nazeevayitsa eta oolitsa
how calls-self this street
What's the name of this street?

Можно осмотреть...?
mawzhna asmatryets
it-is-possible to-look-around
Can we visit...?

...открыт/открыта / ...работает?
atkreet/atkreeta / rabawtayit
open-[m./f.] / works
Is... open?

Когда открывается...?
kagda atkreevayitsa
when opens-self
When does... open?

Где...?
gdye
where
Where is...?

мост	*mawst*	bridge
замок	*zamak*	castle
собор	*sabor*	cathedral
церковь (f.)	*tserkaf ʲi*	church
город	*gawrat*	city, town
экскурсия по городу	*ekskoorsiya pa gawradoo*	city tour
вход / выход	*fkhawt / vweekhat*	entrance / exit
икона	*ikawna*	icon
перекрёсток	*pyiryikryawstak*	intersection
переулок	*pyiryioolak*	lane
карта	*karta*	map
памятник	*pamyitnik*	monument
музей	*moozyey*	museum
дворец	*dvaryets*	palace
дворец культуры	*dvaryets kool ʲitooree*	palace of culture
парк	*park*	park
путь (m.)	*poot ˢ*	path, route
место	*myesta*	place
достопри-мечательности	*dastapri-myichatyil ʲinasti*	places of interest
площадь (f.)	*plawshchat ˢ*	square
стадион	*stadiawn*	stadium
улица	*oolitsa*	street
театр	*tyiatr*	theater
экскурсия	*ekskoorsiya*	tour
светофор	*svyitafor*	traffic lights
университет	*oonivyirsityet*	university
деревня	*dyiryevnya*	village
зоопарк	*zaapark*	zoo

Directions

направо	*naprava*	(on the) right
налево	*nalyeva*	(on the) left

прямо	pr**ya**ma	straight ahead
назад, обратно	naz**a**t, abr**a**tna	back
далеко	dalyik**aw**	far
недалеко, близко	nyidalyik**aw**, bl**i**ska	near
здесь	zdyes**yi**	here
там	tam	there
сразу здесь	sr**a**zoo zdyes**yi**	right here
за углом	za oogl**aw**m	on the corner
напротив	napr**aw**tif	opposite
всё дальше	fsyaw dal**yi**she	further still

Идите прямо до светафора!
*idi**t**ye pr**ya**ma da svyitaf**o**ra*
go-on-foot-[!] straight-ahead to traffic-lights[2]
Walk straight ahead until you reach the traffic lights.

Потом идите налево.
*pat**aw**m idi**t**ye nal**ye**va*
then go-on-foot-[!] left
Then go left.

Поезжайте через мост и потом сверните направо!
*payizhzh**ay**tye chyir**yi**s mawst i pat**aw**m svyir**ni**tye napr**a**va*
go-by-vehicle-[!]-[plural/formal] across bridge[4] and then turn-[!] right
Cross the bridge and then turn right.

Вам надо проехать ещё один километр!
*vam n**a**da pray**e**khat[6] yishch**yaw** ad**i**n kilam**ye**tr*
to-you[3]-[plural/formal] it-is-necessary to-go-through again one kilometer
You need to go another kilometer.

Идите всё время прямо!
*idi**t**ye fsyaw vr**ye**mya pr**ya**ma*
go-on-foot-[!]-[plural/formal] whole time straight
Keep walking straight ahead.

следующая улица
*sly**e**dooy**oo**shchaya **oo**litsa*
next street
The next street.

Покажите это, пожалуйста, на карте!
pakazheetye eta pazhalsta na kartye
show-[!]-[plural/formal] this please on map[6]
Can you show me it on the map, please?

Public Transportation

Russian cities have reliable bus and train systems. All the city districts are accessible by public transportation. Public transportation is also cheap. Buses in particular can be old and cities cover large areas, so make sure you leave plenty of time to get where you're going.

In Moscow or Saint Petersburg, the best way to travel is the metro (subway). Trains run every few minutes and they are very fast. This rapid-transit system was opened by Stalin in the 1930s and has always been a prestigious showcase. The price of a metro ticket will also buy you entrance to a world of almost imperial luxury. The stations are highly ornate, clad in marble, decorated with mosaics, sculptures and murals, and lit by enormous chandeliers.

You can buy travelcards in metro stations. Ask for a metro map at your hotel or an Intourist branch (**У вас есть план метро?** *oo vas yest'e plan myitraw*). It will be useful for finding your own way and for asking people which lines to take.

автобус	*aftawboos*	bus
метро	*myitraw*	metro
трамвай	*tramvay*	tram
троллейбус	*tralyeyboos*	trolleybus
остановка	*astanawfka*	stop

Этот трамвай идёт к…?
etat tramvay idyawt k
this tram goes to...[3]
Does this tram go to...?

прибывать	*pribweevat^s*	arrive (to ~)
идти (II, unidir.)	*itti*	go, walk (to ~)
ехать (multidir.)	*yekhat^s*	go (by vehicle) (to ~)
входить (III)	*fkhadit^s*	go in, get on (a bus/train) (to ~)
выходить (III)	*vweekhadit^s*	go out, get off (a bus/train) (to ~)
отъезжать	*at°yezhzhat^s*	leave (by vehicle) (to ~)

Когда отходит автобус номер...?
kagda atkhawdit aftawboos nawmyir
when leaves bus number
When does bus n°... leave?

Сколько ещё остановок до...?
skawl^[y]ka yishchyaw astanawvak daw
how-many still stops[2] to...[2]
How many more stops until...?

Ещё... остановки.
yishchyaw astanawfki
still... stops[2]
Another... stops.

Скажите, пожалуйста, когда нам выходить?
skazheetye pazhalsta kagda nam vweekhadit^s
tell-[!]-[plural/formal] please when to-us[3] to-get-off
Can you please tell us when we have to get off?

Разрешите пройти!
razryisheetye prayti
permit-[!]-[plural/formal] to-go-through
Let me through, please! (e.g. when getting off a bus or train)

Taxis

такси	*taksi*	taxi
маршрутное такси	*marshrootnaye taksi*	group taxi
стоянка такси	*stayanka taksi*	taxi stand

- Taxis are easily identifiable: the doors, roof and boot are checkered. Here are some tips if you plan to catch taxis:
- Avoid catching taxis from tourist areas (airports, tourist attractions, etc.). You will have little leeway to bargain with the driver and the ride is more than likely to be expensive. Take public transport or walk a few blocks away to hail a taxi. Agree on the price before you get in.
- Private cars also sometimes stop and offer to take you where you want to go for a reasonable price. Weigh up the risk involved. Private cars are best avoided if you are alone or if there are already other people in the car. In Russia as in other countries, tourists are often a target for unscrupulous people.

Вы свободны?
vwee svabawdnee
you-[formal] free-[pl.]
Are you for hire?

ВЫ СВОБОДНЫ?
(Are you for hire?)

Сколько стоит такси до...?
skawl[y]ka stawit taksi da
how-much costs taxi to...?
How much does a taxi cost to...?

... Красной площади?
krasnay plawshchadi
red[2] square[2]
... Red Square?

Я хочу / Мы хотим поехать на/в...
ya khach<u>oo</u> / mwee khat<u>i</u>m pay<u>e</u>khat[s] na/v
I want / we want to-go-by-vehicle to... [4]
I want / We want to go to...

Пожалуйста, остановите здесь/сейчас!
paz<u>ha</u>lsta astanav<u>i</u>tye zdyes[yi]/syich<u>a</u>s
please stop-[!]-[plural/formal] here/now
Stop here/now, please!

TRAVELING BY TRAIN

Trains are a vital form of transportation in a country as vast as Russia. Passengers and goods frequently travel thousands of kilometers to reach their destinations. While these long distances might be a fun adventure for a tourist, for Russians they are an ordinary hassle, especially as rail is the only affordable way to travel for many people.

прибытие	prib<u>wee</u>tiye	arrival
вагон /	vag<u>aw</u>n /	car /
спальный вагон	spal[yi]neey vag<u>aw</u>n	sleeping car
отправление	atpravl<u>ye</u>niye	departure
вагон-ресторан	vag<u>aw</u>n-ryistar<u>a</u>n	dining car
скорый поезд	sk<u>aw</u>reey p<u>aw</u>yist	fast train
справочное бюро	spr<u>a</u>vachnaye byoor<u>aw</u>	information office
камера хранения	k<u>a</u>myira khran<u>ye</u>niya	left luggage
багаж	bag<u>a</u>sh	luggage
бюро	byoor<u>aw</u>	office
платформа / перрон	platf<u>aw</u>rma / pyir<u>aw</u>n	platform
железная дорога	zhel<u>ye</u>znaya dar<u>aw</u>ga	railway
вокзал / станция	vagz<u>a</u>l / st<u>a</u>ntseeya	railway station / station
касса	k<u>a</u>ssa	ticket booth

сто двадцать пять

путь	pootˢ	track
поезд	pawyist	train
расписание поездов	raspisaniye payizdawf	train timetable
зал ожидания	zal azheedaniya	waiting room

For short distances and suburban destinations, you'll take the **электричка** *ilyiktrichka* (literally: "the electric"). Comfort is basic.

Сколько стоит билет до...?
skawl⁽ʸ⁾ka stawit bilyet da
how-much costs ticket to...?
How much does a ticket to... cost?

Когда приезжает поезд из...?
kagda priyizzhayit pawyist iz
when comes train from...?
When does the train from... arrive?

билет	bilyet	ticket
обратный билет	abratneey bilyet	return ticket
туда и обратно	tooda i abratna	round trip (i.e. there and back)
мягкий вагон	myakhkiy vagawn	1st class
жёсткий вагон	zhawstkiy vagawn	2nd class
резервирование	ryizyirviravaniye	reservation
плацкарта	platskarta	reservation slip
опоздание	apazdaniye	delay
точно	tawchna	on time

The Moscow-Vladivostok line, more commonly known as the Trans-Siberian, is one of the world's legendary train journeys. It is one of the last survivors of the golden age of rail. The journey is an adventure. It takes a week to cover all 9,500 km of the world's longest railway line.

There is a **проводник** *pravadnik*, *conductor (he)* or **проводница** *pravadnitsa*, *conductor (she)* in every car to look after passengers. Every morning he comes around to fold back the berths, adjust the heating and bring you hot water for tea. You soon get to know the other passengers – even for Russians, a trip on the "Trans-Sib" is something special. People often share the food they have brought with them with their fellow passengers and start chatting.

Поезд опаздывает?
pawyist apazdeevayit
train is-late
Is the train running late?

Нужно сделать пересадку?
noozhna zdyelat⁸ pyiryisatkoo
it-is-necessary to-do change⁴
Do we/I have to change (trains)?

Этот поезд на...?
etat pawyist na
this train to...⁴
Is this the train to...?

Где останавливается поезд?
gdye astanavlivayitsa pawyist
where stops-self train
Where does the train stop?

Сколько времени длится путешествие до...?
skawlʸika vryemyini dlitsa pootyishestviye da
how-much time² lasts journey to...²
How long is the journey to...?

Здесь есть ещё свободное место?
zdyesʸi yest⁸ yishchyaw svabawdnaye myesta
here there-is still free place
Is there a spare seat here?

Извините, пожалуйста, это моё место.
izvinitye pazhalsta eta mayaw myesta
excuse-[!] please this my place
Excuse me, this is my seat.

сто двадцать семь

Можно открыть/закрыть дверь/окно?
mawzhna atkreet⁸/zakreet⁸ dvyer⁽ʸ⁾/aknaw
it-is-possible to-open/to-close door[4]/window[4]
May I/we open/close the door/window?

Мне холодно/жарко.
mnye khawladna/zharka
to-me[3] cold/hot
I'm cold/hot.

Можно получить чай/одеяло?
mawzhna paloochit⁸ chay/adyiyala
it-is-possible to-receive tea[4]/blanket[4]
Could I/we have some tea / a blanket?

Я хочу получить чистый комплект белья.
ya khachoo paloochit⁸ chyisteey kamplyekt byil'ya
I want to-receive clean[4] set[4] linen[2]
Could I have a clean set of sheets?

Я хочу поднять/опустить полку.
ya khachoo padnyat⁸/apoostit⁸ pawlkoo
I want to-raise/to-lower shelf[4]
I want to put the berth up/down.

TRAVELING BY CAR

We strongly advise against driving to Russia in your own car, especially if you have never been to Russia before. If you are undeterred, always take the shortest route and gather as much information about itineraries as you can before you leave from a travel agency or automobile association. Make sure you correctly evaluate distances. Always check the scale on your road map.
• When you enter Russia, have the customs officer check the condition of your vehicle (any bumps or scratches). Otherwise you could have problems leaving again.

- Be warned that there is a good chance of your windscreen wipers, antenna and hubcaps being stolen.

(авто)машина	(afta)mash<u>ee</u>na	car
автопринцеп-дача	aftaprints<u>e</u>p-d<u>a</u>cha	caravan
ехать дальше	yekhat^s dal^{yi}she	continue (to ~)
шофёр, водитель	shaf<u>yaw</u>r, vadi<u>tye</u>l^{yi}	driver
водительское удостоверение	vadi<u>tyi</u>l^{yi}skaye oodastavy<u>i</u>r<u>e</u>niye	driver's licence
ехать обратно	yekhat^s abr<u>a</u>tna	go back (to ~)
автофургон-дача, жилой автомобиль	aftafoorg<u>aw</u>n-d<u>a</u>cha, zhel<u>oy</u> aftamabi<u>l</u>^{yi}	mobile home
автомагистраль	aftamagistr<u>a</u>l^{yi}	motorway, highway
поставить машину (III, perf.)	pas<u>ta</u>vit^s mash<u>ee</u>noo	park a car (to ~)
автостоянка	aftasta<u>ya</u>nka	parking
стоянка автомашин	sta<u>ya</u>nka aftamash<u>ee</u>n	parking space
регистрационный документ	ryigistratsee<u>yaw</u>neey dakoom<u>ye</u>nt	registration papers
дорога, главная дорога	dar<u>aw</u>ga, gl<u>a</u>vnaya dar<u>aw</u>ga	road, main road
охраняемая автостоянка	akhran<u>ya</u>yimaya aftasta<u>ya</u>nka	security parking
улица	<u>oo</u>litsa	street
повернуть (perf.)	pavyirn<u>oo</u>t^s	turn (to ~)

Сколько километров до ближайшего города?
sk<u>aw</u>l^{yi}ka kilam<u>ye</u>traf da blizh<u>ay</u>sheva g<u>aw</u>rada
how-many kilometers[2] to nearest[2] town[2]
How many kilometers to the next town?

В гостинице есть гараж?
v-gast<u>i</u>nitse yest^s gar<u>a</u>sh
in hotel[6] there-is garage
Does the hotel have parking?

Где ближайшая автостоянка?
gdye blizhayshaya aftastayanka
where nearest parking
Where is the nearest parking lot?

ГДЕ БЛИЖАЙШАЯ АВТОСТОЯНКА?
(Where is the nearest parking lot?)

Road Signs

внимание	vnimaniye	caution
объезд	ab°yest	detour
проезд запрещён	prayest zapryishchyawn	no entry
улица с односторонним движением	oolitsa s-adnastarawnnim dvizheniyem	one-way street
открыто / закрыто	atkreeta / zakreeta	open / closed
переход	pyiryikhawt	pedestrian crossing
ремонтные работы	ryimawntneeye rabawtee	roadwork
стоп	stawp	stop

Most road signs in Russia are international. However, roads and signage are not always well maintained. Road markings in particular are often nonexistent. Be more careful than usual and avoid driving at night.

At the Service Station

дизель	dizyel[yi]	diesel
дистиллированная вода	distil<u>ir</u><u>aw</u>vannaya vad<u>a</u>	distilled water
моторное масло	mat<u>aw</u>rnaye m<u>a</u>sla	engine oil
автозаправка	aftazapr<u>a</u>fka	gas / petrol station
бензин	byinz<u>i</u>n	gasoline / petrol
заправлять	zaprav<u>l</u>yat[s]	get gasoline (to ~)
канистра	kan<u>i</u>stra	jerrican
АИ 93	a-i dyivyin<u>aw</u>sta-tri	93-octane gasoline
АИ 95	a-i dyivyin<u>aw</u>sta-pyat[s]	95-octane gasoline
АИ 98	a-i dyivyin<u>aw</u>sta-v<u>aw</u>syim[yi]	98-octane unleaded gasoline
бензопункт	byinzap<u>oo</u>nkt	service station
давление воздуха	davl<u>ye</u>niye v<u>aw</u>zdookha	tire pressure

It can be hard to find unleaded gasoline in small towns and villages in Russia. Diesel is easy to find. Since service stations are few and far between, always keep an extra jerrican of fuel with you.

Пожалуйста, полный бак!
pazh<u>a</u>lsta p<u>aw</u>lneey bak
please full tank
Fill her up, please!

Breakdowns

ГИБДД	gibed<u>e</u>de	State Automobile Inspectorate

ГИБДД *gibed<u>e</u>de* (Государственная Инспекция Безопасности Дорожного Движения *gasood<u>a</u>rstvennaya insp<u>ye</u>ktsiya byizap<u>a</u>snasti dar<u>aw</u>zhnava dvizh<u>e</u>niya*) is the Russian highway patrol. They enforce the road rules (remember it is compulsory to wear a seat belt), but also provide assistance when vehicles break down, and write accident reports. *GIBDD* officers patrol the main roads.

авторемонт / авторемонтная мастерская	aftaryim<u>aw</u>nt / aftaryim<u>aw</u>ntnaya mastyirskaya	auto repairs / garage
авария	av<u>a</u>riya	breakdown
срочный ремонт	sr<u>aw</u>chneey ryim<u>aw</u>nt	express repairs
страхование	strakhav<u>a</u>niye	insurance
домкрат	damkr<u>a</u>t	jack
ремонт	ryim<u>aw</u>nt	repairs
запасная часть / запчасть	zap<u>a</u>snaya chast[s] / zapch<u>a</u>st[s]	spare part
буксировочный трос	books<u>i</u>ravachneey traws	tow cable
буксирный автомобиль	books<u>i</u>rneey aftamabi<u>l</u>[y]	tow truck

У моей машины прокол шины.
oo may<u>e</u>y mash<u>ee</u>nee prak<u>aw</u>l sh<u>ee</u>nee
with my[2] car[2] puncture of-tire[2]
My car has a flat tire.

Вы можете это сделать?
vwee m<u>aw</u>zhetye <u>e</u>ta zdyelat[s]
you-[formal/plural] can this to-do-[perf.]
Can you fix it?

132 сто тридцать два

Вы можете отбуксировать машину в ближайший авторемонт?
vwee mawzhetye atbooksiravat⁸ masheenoo v-blizhaysheey aftaryimawnt
you-[formal/plural] can to-tow car⁴ to nearest garage
Can you tow my car to the nearest garage?

Сколько времени продлится ремонт?
skawl[y]ka vryemyini pradlitsa ryimawnt
how-much time² will-last repairs
How long will the repairs take?

У вас есть официальная запчасть?
oo vas yest⁸ afitseeal[y]naya zapchast⁸
in-the-possession of-you²-[formal/plural] there-is official spare-part
Do you have the OEM spare part?

A good precaution is to find other tourists to travel with you and share the driving. Many Russian roads are in such bad condition that it's a good idea to carry a toolkit and some essential spare parts with you.

Road Accidents

скорая помощь (f.)	*skawraya pawmashch'*	ambulance
врач	*vrach*	doctor
дорожное происшествие / авария	*darawzhnaye praishestviye / avariya*	road accident

Мы попали в аварию.
mwee papali v-avariyoo
we hit into accident
We've had an accident.

Пожалуйста, позвоните/вызовите скорую помощь!
pazhalsta pazvanitye/vweezavitye skawrooyoo pawmashch'
please telephone-[!]/call-out-[!]-[formal/plural] fast⁴ help⁴
Please call an ambulance!

Пожалуйста, напишите ваше имя и адрес!
pazhalsta napisheetye vashe imya i adryis
please write-[!]-[formal/plural] your name and address
Please write your name and address!

Я (не) виновен/виновна.
ya (nyi) vinawvyin/vinawvna
I (not) at-fault-[m./f.]
I'm (not) at fault.

У меня свидетели!
oo myinya svidyetyili
in-the-possession of-me² witnesses
I have witnesses!

Most drivers in Russia do not have insurance. Therefore, if you are involved in an accident, always call out the **ГИБДД** *gibedede*, *the highway patrol*, to fill out a report. As a foreign visitor, you must insure your vehicle at the border when you enter Russia.

TRAVELING BY PLANE OR BOAT

Traveling by Plane

If you are traveling alone, you will save a lot of time by booking your flights through **Интурист**, *Intourist*, a travel agency specialized in travel to Russia. However, Intourist branches are not always easy to find outside of major hotels. For domestic flights, departures are frequently delayed. Passengers may be kept waiting until any spare seats are filled or until the ground staff get around to refueling the aircraft. Flights reserved as part of a group package usually run closer to schedule.

авиалиния	*avialiniya*	airline
аэропорт	*airapawrt*	airport
лететь (III, unidir.)	*lyityet ˢ*	fly (to ~)
самолёт	*samalyawt*	plane (self-fly)
авиабилет	*aviabilyet*	plane ticket
стартовать	*startavat ˢ*	start the engines (to ~)

стюардесса	*styooard**e**sa*	stewardess
вылетать	*vweelyit**a**t*[8]	take off (to ~)

Мне плохо.
*mnye pl**aw**kha*
to-me[2] bad
I don't feel well.

Когда самолёт пойдёт на посадку?
*kagd**a** samal**yaw**t payd**yaw**t na pas**a**tkoo*
when plan will-go to landing[4]
When does the plane land?

Traveling by Boat

корабль, судно	*kar**a**bl*[yi], *s**oo**dna*	boat, ship
экскурсия	*iksk**oo**rsiya*	cruise
теплоход	*tyiplakh**aw**t*	diesel-powered boat
паром	*par**aw**m*	ferry
экскурсия по порту	*iksk**oo**rsiya pa p**aw**rtoo*	harbor cruise
остров	*<u>aw</u>straf*	island
земля	*zyiml**ya***	land
озеро	*<u>aw</u>zyira*	lake
порт	*pawrt*	port, harbor
река	*ryik**a***	river
море	*m**aw**rye*	sea
берег	*b**ye**rik*	shore, bank
лодка	*l**aw**tka*	small boat, rowboat
пароход	*parakh**aw**t*	steamship
вода	*vad**a***	water
пристань	*pr**i**stan*[yi]	wharf

Когда прибудет судно?
*kagd**a** prib**oo**dyit s**oo**dna*
when will-arrive boat
When does the boat come in?

Когда отплывает теплоход?
*kagd**a** atpleev**a**yit tyiplakh**aw**t*
when swims-out boat
When does the boat leave?

КОГДА ПРИБУДЕТ СУДНО?
(When does the boat come in?)

ACCOMMODATION AND MEALS

At the Hotel

гостиница	gastinitsa	hotel
мотель	matyel^{yi}	motel

Где можно переночевать?
gdye m<u>a</u>wzhna pyiryinachyiva<u>t</u>^s
where it-is-possible to-spend-night
Where can I/we spend the night?

Я заказал/заказала одноместный/двухместный номер.
ya zakaz<u>a</u>l / zakaz<u>a</u>la adnamy<u>e</u>sneey/dvookhmy<u>e</u>sneey n<u>a</u>wmyir
I ordered-[m./f.] one-place/two-place number
I booked a single/double room.

Мне нужен номер на сутки.
mnye n<u>oo</u>zhen n<u>a</u>wmyir na s<u>oo</u>tki
to-me³ it-is-necessary number for 24-hour-period⁴
I need a room for one night.

... на две ночи.
na dvye nawchi
for two[4] nights[2]
... for two nights.

Завтрак включён в эту цену?
zaftrak fklyoochawn v-etoo tsenoo
breakfast included in that[4] price[4]
Is breakfast included in that price?

Можно посмотреть номер?
mawzhna pasmatryet⁵ nawmyir
it-is-possible to-see number[4]
Can I/we see the room?

Я хочу номер с душем / другой номер.
ya khachoo nawmyir z-dooshem / droogoy nawmyir
I want number with shower[5] / other number
I want a room with a shower / a different room.

ванная	*vannaya*	bathroom
кровать (f.)	*kravat⁵*	bed
одеяло	*adyiyala*	blanket
холодная вода	*khalawdnaya vada*	cold water
столовая	*stalawvaya*	dining room, cafeteria
этаж	*itash*	floor
первый этаж	*pyerveey itash*	ground floor
горячая вода	*garyachaya vada*	hot water
ключ	*klyooch*	key
прачечная	*prachyichnaya*	laundry (place)
багаж	*bagash*	luggage
служба приёма, администрация	*sloozhba priyawma, administratseeya*	reception
номер, комната	*nawmyir, kawmnata*	room
обслуживание	*apsloozheevaniye*	service
душ	*doosh*	shower
полотенце	*palatyentse*	towel

N.B. In Russia, the ground floor is called the *first floor*: **первый этаж** *pyerveey itash*.

Во сколько завтрак/обед/ужин?
va-skawl^{yi}ka zaftrak/abyet/oozheen
at how-many breakfast/lunch/dinner
What time is breakfast/lunch/dinner?

Телевизор/лампа не работает.
tyilyivizar/lampa nyi rabawtayit
television/lamp not works
The television / the lamp doesn't work.

Мне надо уезжать.
mnye nada ooyizhzhat^s
to-me[3] it-is-necessary to-leave
I have to leave.

Когда я должен/должна заплатить?
kagda ya dawlzhen/dalzhna zaplatit^s
when I must-[m./f.] to-pay
When should I pay?

предварительно	сейчас	в день отъезда
pryidvarityil^{yi}na	*syichas*	*v-dyen^{yi} at^{o}yezda*
in advance	now	when you leave

Разбудите меня, пожалуйста, в... завтра утром!
razbooditye myinya pazhalsta v zaftra ootram
wake-[!]-[perf.] me[2] please at tomorrow in-the-morning
Can you please wake me at... tomorrow morning?

Camping

рюкзак	*ryookzak*	backpack
кемпинг	*kyemping*	camp site
питьевая вода	*pit^{s}ivaya vada*	drinking water

турбаза	toorb__a__za	holiday village
спальный мешок	spal[ly]neey myish__aw__k	sleeping bag
палатка	pal__a__tka	tent
умывальная	oomweeval[ly]naya	washroom

Где можно поставить палатку / приготовить еду?
gdye m__aw__zhna past__a__vit⁵ pal__a__tkoo / prigat__aw__vit⁵ yed__oo__
where it-is possible to-put-[perf.] tent⁴ / to-prepare-[perf.] food⁴
Where can I/we pitch our tent / cook?

At the Restaurant

завтрак / завтракать	z__a__ftrak / z__a__ftrakat⁵	breakfast / to have breakfast
обед / обедать	ab__ye__t / ab__ye__dat⁵	lunch / to have lunch
ужин / ужинать	__oo__zheen / __oo__zheenat⁵	dinner / to have dinner

нож	n__aw__sh	knife
вилка	v__i__lka	fork
ложка	l__aw__shka	spoon
тарелка	tar__ye__lka	plate
чашка	ch__a__shka	cup
стакан	stak__a__n	glass

меню	miny__oo__	menu
закуски	zak__oo__ski	appetizers
главное блюдо	gl__a__vnaye bly__oo__da	main course
десерт	dyis__ye__rt	dessert

бар	bar	bar
кафе	kaf__e__	café
столовая	stal__aw__vaya	cafeteria
кабак	kab__a__k	dive, tavern
пельменная	pyil[ly]my__e__nnaya	pelmeni (Russian ravioli) bar

ресторан	ryistar*a*n	restaurant
закусочная	zak*oo*sachnaya	snack bar
буфет	boof*ye*t	stand-up snack bar
кондитерская	kand*i*tirskaya	sweet shop / tea room
чайная	ch*a*ynaya	tea room / coffee shop

Some hotels have a **шведский стол** shv*ye*tskiy stawl (literally: "Swedish table"), meaning a *smorgasbord*. You can eat as much as you want. You must pay extra for drinks.

Официант!	**Девушка!**	**Будьте добры...!**
afits*a*nt	d*ye*vooshka	boot^stye dabr*ee*
Waiter!	young-woman	be-[!] kind
	Miss!	Would you mind...?

If a waiter or waitress goes past your table, it is not impolite to ask: **Кто обслуживает этот стол?** ktaw apsl*oo*zheevayit *e*tat stawl, Who is serving this table?

Здесь свободно?	**Я голоден/голодна.**
zdyes^{yi} svab*aw*dna	ya g*aw*ladyin/galadn*a*
here free	I hungry-[m./f.]
Is this table free?	I'm hungry.

• Russian Culinary Specialities

беляши	byilyish*ee*	belyashi: buns stuffed with meatballs (a Tatar speciality)
борщ	bawrshch	borscht: beetroot soup (contains other vegetables and often meat)
чебуреки	chyiboor*ye*ki	chebureki: chunky ravioli stuffed with lamb (a Caucasian speciality)
голубцы	galoopts*ee*	golubtsi: cabbage leaves stuffed with rice and minced meat

окрошка	a*kraw*shka	okroshka: cold summer soup made of kvas, diced meat, egg, cucumber and fermented milk
пельмени	pyil^{yi}*myen*i	pelmeni: ravioli filled with meat and served with sour cream (a Siberian speciality)
плов	plawf	pilaf: rice mixed with lamb (a Central Asian speciality)
пончики	*pawn*chiki	ponchiki: little dumplings sometimes filled with jam
рассольник	ra*sawl*^{yi}nik	rassolnik: meat and pickled cucumber soup
шашлык	shash*leek*	shashlik: kebab (a Caucasian speciality)
солянка	sa*lyan*ka	solyanka: spicy fish or meat soup

Note! **Котлеты** katl*yet*ee are not cutlets! They are *meatballs or croquettes made of meat and breadcrumbs,* and sometimes herbs.

Что вы можете нам посоветовать?
shtaw vwee mawzhetye nam pasavyetavat^s
what you-[formal/plural] can to-us³ to-advise-[perf.]
What do you recommend?

Я вегетарианец/вегетарианка.
ya vyigyitarianyits/vyigyitarianka
I vegetarian-[m./f.]
I'm a vegetarian.

Принесите, пожалуйста, одну порцию / две порции...
prinyisitye pazhalsta adnoo pawrtseeyoo / dvye pawrtseei
bring-[!] please one⁴ portion⁴ / two⁴ portions²
Could you please bring us a portion / two portions (of)...

сто сорок один **141**

Что это?
shtaw eta
what that
What is this?

Это очень вкусно.
eta awchyin[yi] fkoosna
this very tasty
It's very tasty.

Хорошо, возьмём!
kharashaw vaz[yi]myawm
good we-will-take
Good. We'll take it!

Приятного аппетита!
priyatnava apyitita
pleasant[2] appetite[2]
Bon appétit! / Enjoy your meal!

Пожалуйста, счёт!
pazhalsta shchyawt
please check/bill
Check/bill, please!

Это мясное блюдо?
eta myisnoye blyooda
this meat dish
Is it a meat dish?

Я возьму два шашлыка.
vaz[yi]moo dva shashleeka
I-will-take two shashlik[2]
I'll take two shashliks.

Спасибо, вам тоже!
spasiba vam tawzhe
thanks to-you[3]-[formal/plural] too
Thank you. Same to you!

Сколько с меня?
skawl[yi]ka s-myinya
how-much from me[2]
How much do I owe you?

It is customary to leave a **чаевые** *chayivweeye*, *tip*, equal to around 10% or 15% of the check. You can say to the waiter/waitress, **Это для вас!** *eta dlya vas*, *That's for you!*

• Drinks

безалкогольные напитки	*byizalkagawl[yi]neeye napitki*	non-alcoholic drinks
какао	*kakaaw*	cocoa
кофе	*kawfye*	coffee
сироп	*sirawp*	cordial

фруктовый сок	_frooktawvweey sawk_	fruit juice
лимонад	_limanat_	lemonade
квас	_kvas_	kvas*
молоко	_malakaw_	milk
чай	_chay_	tea
~ с молоком	_s-malakawm_	~ with milk
~ с сахаром	_s-sakharam_	~ with sugar
~ без сахара	_byis-sakhara_	~ without sugar
вода (минеральная ~)	_vada (minyiral[y]naya)_	water (mineral ~)

* **Квас** _kvas_ is a sour fermented drink made from rye flour and malt.

алкогольные напитки	_alkagawl[y]neeye napitki_	alcoholic drinks
пиво	_piva_	beer
шампанское	_shampanskaye_	champagne
коктейль	_kaktyeyl[y]_	cocktail
коньяк	_kan[y]yak_	cognac, brandy
джин	_dzheen_	gin
ром	_rawm_	rum
водка (со льдом)	_vawtka (sa-l[y]dawm)_	vodka (with ice)
вино	_vinaw_	wine
красное ~	_krasnaye_	red ~
белое ~	_byelaye_	white ~

Although genuine French champagne is highly appreciated in Russia and Russians have become one of the world's biggest consumers of champagne, the word **шампанское** _shampanskaye_ more commonly refers to local sparkling wine. Russian sparkling wines tend to be very sweet.

одна чашка чая/кофе
adna chashka chaya/kawfye
one cup of-tea[2]/of-coffee[2]
a cup of tea/coffee

один стакан вина/сока
adin stakan vina/sawka
one glass of-wine[2]/of-juice[2]
a glass of wine/juice

одна бутылка вина/водки
adna booteelka vina/vawtki
one bottle of-wine[2]/of-vodka[2]
a bottle of wine/vodka

три кружки пива
tri krooshki piva
three mug[2] of-beer[2]
three mugs of beer

Мне хочется пить.
mnye khawchyitsa pit[s]
to-me[3] it-wants-self to-drink
I'm thirsty.

За ваше здоровье!
za vashe zdarawv[y]ye
for your[4] health[4]
To your health! / Cheers!

За здоровье!
za zdarawv[y]ye
for health[4]
Cheers!

SHOPPING

булочная	*boolashnaya*	bakery
книжный магазин	*knizhneey magazin*	bookstore
универмаг	*oonivyirmak*	department store
продовольственный магазин / гастроном	*pradawl[y]stvyineey magazin / gastranawm*	grocery store
киоск	*kiawsk*	kiosk
рынок	*reenak*	market
магазин сувениров	*magazin soovyiniraf*	souvenir store
магазин	*magazin*	store
супермаркет	*soopyirmarkyit*	supermarket

ГУМ *goom*, in Moscow, is one of the world's most beautiful shopping arcades, built in the nineteeth century. **ГУМ** is short for **Государственный Универсальный Магазин** *gasoodarstv[y]neey oonivyirsal[y]neey magazin*, State Universal Shop.

Я хочу пойти купить что-нибудь.
ya khachoo payti koopit[s] shtaw-niboot[s]
I want to-go to-buy something[4]
I'd like to go shopping.

144   сто сорок четыре

Где можно купить/получить...?
*gdye m**aw**zhna koop**it**ˢ/palooch**it**ˢ*
where it-is-possible to-buy/to-receive...⁴
Where can I/we buy/get (for free)...?

Магазин открыт/закрыт?
*magaz**in** atkr**eet**/zakr**eet***
shop open/closed
Is the shop open/closed?

Even if shortages are a thing of the past in Russia, queues have not completely disappeared. If you have to wait in line, ask the following question:

Сколько мне ждать?
*sk**awl**ʸⁱka mnye zhdatˢ*
how-much to-me³ to-wait
How long will I have to wait?

сигареты	*sigar**ye**tee*	cigarettes
карта города	*k**a**rta g**aw**rada*	city map
компакт-диск	*kamp**a**kt disk*	compact disc
словарь	*slav**ar**ʸⁱ*	dictionary
газета	*gaz**ye**ta*	newspaper
карандаш	*karand**a**sh*	pencil
дорожная карта	*dar**aw**zhnaya k**a**rta*	road map

Что ещё желаете?
*shtaw yishch**yaw** zhel**a**yitye*
what still you-wish-[formal/plural]
Would you like anything else?

Ещё больше...
*yishch**yaw** b**awl**ʸⁱshe*
still more
Some more...

Сколько стоит...?
*sk**awl**ʸⁱka st**aw**it*
how-much costs
How much does... cost?

Это (очень) дорого.
*eta (**aw**chyinʸⁱ) d**aw**raga*
that (very) dear
That's (very) expensive.

ЧТО ЕЩЁ ЖЕЛАЕТЕ?
(Would you like anything else?)

Я хочу просто посмотреть.
ya khachoo prawsta pasmatryet⁸
I want simply to-look
I'd just like to look.

Можно попробовать/примереть?
mawzhna paprawbavat⁸/primyeryit⁸
it-is-possible to-try/to-measure
May I/we taste / try this on?

Дайте мне, пожалуйста, открытку.
daytye mnye pazhalsta atkreetkoo
give-[!] to-me³ please postcard⁴
I'll take a postcard, please.

Я ищу газету.
ya ishchoo gazyetoo
I seek newspaper⁴
I'm looking for a newspaper.

Food and Spices

яблоко	_ya_blaka	apple
говядина	gav_ya_dina	beef
хлеб	khl_ye_p	bread
булочка	_boo_lachka	bun / bread roll
масло	_ma_sla	butter / oil
торт	tawrt	cake
икра	ikr_a_	caviar
икра (чёрная ~)	ikr_a_ (ch_aw_rnaya)	caviar (black ~)*
икра (красная ~)	ikr_a_ (kr_a_snaya)	caviar (red ~)*
сыр	seer	cheese
курица	_koo_ritsa	chicken
печенье	pyich_ye_n'ye	cookies / biscuits
сливки (pl.)	_sli_fki	cream
яйцо	_yay_tsa	egg
рыба	_ree_ba	fish
фрукты (pl.)	_froo_ktee	fruit
гуляш	gool_ya_sh	goulash
мёд	myawt	honey
мороженое	mar_aw_zhenaye	ice cream
варенье	var_ye_n'ye	jam
мясо	m_ya_sa	meat
котлеты	katl_ye_tee	meatballs
молоко	malak_aw_	milk
грибы	grib_wee_	mushrooms
горчица	g_a_rchitsa	mustard
перец	p_ye_ryits	pepper
пирог	pir_aw_k	pie
картофель (f.)	kart_aw_fyil^{yi}	potato
птица	pt_i_tsa	poultry
рис	ris	rice
жаркое	zhark_oy_e	roast
ромштекс	ramsht_ye_ks	rump steak
соль (f.)	sawl^{yi}	salt

сто сорок семь   147

колбаса	*kalbas̲a*	sausage
шницель	*shnitselʸⁱ*	schnitzel
суп	*soop*	soup
сахар	*s̲akhar*	sugar
овощи	*a̲wvashchi*	vegetables

* Only "black caviar" comes from sturgeon eggs. "Red caviar" is roe from other types of fish (mainly salmon) and is much cheaper.

Я это беру.
ya e̲ta byiroo̲
I this take
I'll take this.

Я это не возьму.
ya e̲ta nyi vazʸⁱmoo̲
I this not will-take
I won't take this.

Это всё. / Это хорошо.
e̲ta fsyaw / e̲ta kharasha̲w
that all / that good
That's all. / That's good.

Достаточно.
dasta̲tachna
That's enough.

Мне нужно сто граммов сыра.
mnye noo̲zhna staw gra̲mmaf se̲era
to-me³ is-necessary 100 grams² of-cheese²
I need 100 grams of cheese.

AT THE BANK

банк	*bank*	bank
банкнота	*bankna̲wta*	banknote
пункт обмена валюты	*poonkt abmye̲na valyoo̲tee*	bureau de change
наличные деньги	*nali̲chneeye dyenʸⁱgi*	cash
обменять деньги	*abmyinya̲tᵉ dyenʸⁱgi*	change money (to ~)
кредитная карта	*kryidi̲tnaya ka̲rta*	credit card
валюта	*valyoo̲ta*	currency
курс	*koors*	exchange rate
мелочь	*myela̲chʸⁱ*	small change

Госбанк (Государственный банк)	*gawsbank (gasood<u>a</u>rstvyineey bank)*	State Bank (central bank)
туристический чек	*toorist<u>i</u>chyiskiy chek*	traveler's check

N.B. **банк** *bank* means *bank*, but **банка** *b<u>a</u>nka* means *jar* or *can*.

Можно здесь обменять валюту/деньги?
m<u>a</u>wzhna zdyes^{yi} abmimyn<u>ya</u>t^s valy<u>oo</u>too/dyen^{yi}gi?
it-is-possible here to-change currency[4]/money[4]
Can we/I change currency/money here?

Currencies

	1	2-4, 22-24, etc.	5-20, 25-30, etc.
Ruble	**рубль** *roobl^{yi}*	**рубля** *roobl<u>ya</u>*	**рублей** *roobly<u>ey</u>*
Kopeck	**копейка** *kap<u>ye</u>yka*	**копейки** *kap<u>ye</u>yki*	**копеек** *kap<u>ye</u>yik*

(See also **Counting**)

Сколько рублей я получу за...?
sk<u>a</u>wl^{yi}ka roobly<u>ey</u> ya pal<u>oo</u>choo za
how-many rubles[2] I will-receive-[perf.] for
How many rubles will I get for...?

сто долларов	*staw d<u>a</u>wlaraf*	100 dollars
сто фунтов (стерлингов)	*staw f<u>oo</u>ntaf (st<u>ye</u>rlingaf)*	100 pounds (sterling)
сто евро	*staw y<u>e</u>vra*	100 euros

Мне надо обменять сто долларов.
mnye n<u>a</u>da abmiyn<u>ya</u>t^s staw d<u>a</u>wlaraf
to-me[3] it-is-necessary to-change 100[4] dollars[2]
I'd like to change $100.

AT THE POST OFFICE

Мне нужно отправить это письмо / эту посылку...
mnye noozhna atpravit⁽ˢ⁾ eta pis⁽ʸⁱ⁾maw / etoo paseelkoo
to-me[3] it-is-necessary to-send this letter / this parcel
I'd like to send this letter / this parcel...

... в Америку/Англию/Австралию/Канаду.
v-amyerikoo/angliyoo/afstraliyoo/kanadoo
to America[4]/England[4]/Australia[4]/Canada[4]
... to America/England/Australia/Canada.

Дайте мне, пожалуйста, бланк для телеграммы (за границу).
daytye mnye pazhalsta blank dlya tyilyigrammwee (za granitsoo)
give-[!] to-me[3] please form for telegram[2] (across border[4])
Could you please give me a form for an (international) telegram?

адрес	*adryis*	address
авиапочта	*aviapawchta*	airmail
конверт	*kanvyert*	envelope
бланк	*blank*	form
письмо	*pis⁽ʸⁱ⁾maw*	letter
почтовый ящик	*pachtawvweey yashchik*	mail box
пакет	*pakyet*	parcel
открытка	*atkreetka*	postcard
почта, почтовое отделение	*pawchta, pachtawvaye atdyilyeniye*	post office
отправитель	*atpravityel⁽ʸⁱ⁾*	sender
бандероль	*banderawl⁽ʸⁱ⁾*	small parcel (for printed matter)
марка (почтовая ~)	*marka (pachtawvaya ~)*	stamp (postage ~)
приём телеграмм	*priyawm tyilyigram*	telegram counter

USING THE TELEPHONE

код назначения	kawt naznachyeniya	area code (code destination)
разговор	razgavawr	call, conversation
позвонить (по телефону)	pazvanit^s (paw tyilyifawnoo)	call (to ~) (by phone)
международный разговор	myezhdoonarawdneey razgavawr	international call
местный разговор	myestneey razgavawr	local call
коммутатор	kamootatar	operator
телефон-автомат	tyilyifawn-aftamat	pay phone (telephone-automat)
телеграф	tyilyigraf	telegraph
телефон	tyilyifawn	telephone
телефонный разговор	tyilyifawnneey razgavawr	telephone conversation
номер телефона	nawmyir tyilyifawna	telephone number

You can make phone calls from the post office and from public pay phones in the street. However, some phones are for inter-city calls only.

Где можно позвонить по телефону?
gdye mawzhna pazvanit^s pa tyilyifawnoo
where it-is-possible to-call by telephone[3]
Where can I/we make a phone call?

Напишите мне номер телефона / код назначения...
napisheetye mnye nawmyir tyilyifawna / kawt naznachyeniya
write-[!] for-me[4] number of-telephone[2] / code of-destination[2]
Can you please write the phone number / the area code for... for me?

Я хочу заказать разговор с Лондоном.
ya khachoo zakazat^s razgavawr s-lawndanam
I want to-order call with London[6]
I would like to place a call to London.

сто пятьдесят один

Мне надо долго ждать?
mnye nada dawlga zhdat[8]
to-me[3] it-is-necessary long to-wait
Will I have to wait long?

Номер не отвечает.
nawmyir nyi atvyichayit
number not answers
The number isn't answering.

Занято!
zanyita
It's busy/engaged.

Алло?
alaw
Hello?

Лондон – вторая кабина пожалуйста!
lawndan ftaraya kabina pazhalsta
London – second booth please!

Джон у телефона.
dzhawn oo tyilyifawna
John at phone
It's John here.

С кем я говорю?
s-kyem ya gavaryoo
with whom[5] I speak
Who's speaking?

Мне нужен господин... / нужна госпожа...
mnye noozhen gaspadin / noozhna gaspazha
to-me[3] is-necessary Mr / is-necessary Miss/Mrs
I would like to speak to Mr.../Miss.../Mrs...

FORMALITIES

Filling Out a Form

If you are traveling in a group, the group leader will fill out all the forms. For independent travelers, here are the most common words you will encounter on forms, plus some handy expressions.

Мне нужна виза на...
mnye noozhna viza na
to-me³ is-necessary-[f.] visa for
I need a visa for...

Это возможно?
eta vazmawzhna
that is-possible
Is that possible?

Я могу подождать?
ya magoo padazhdat^s
I can to-wait
Can I wait?

адрес	*adryis*	address
приезд	*priyest*	arrival (date of ~)
отъезд	*at°yest*	departure (date of ~)
въезд	*v°yest*	entry (date of ~)
выезд	*vweeyest*	exit (date of ~)
имя	*imya*	first name
бланк	*blank*	form
право	*prava*	legal right
паспорт	*paspart*	passport
местожительство	*myestazheetyel^{yi}stva*	place of residence
подпись (f.)	*pawtpis^{yi}*	signature
улица	*oolitsa*	street
фамилия	*familiya*	surname

Я хочу ещё остаться на два дня / на неделю.
ya khachoo yishchyaw astatsa na dva dnya / na nyidyelyoo
I want still to-stop-self for two⁴ days² / for week⁴
I'd like to stay another two days / another week.

Мне надо лететь / ехать уже завтра.
mnye nada lyityet^s / yekhat^s oozhe zaftra
to-me³ is-necessary to-fly / to-go already tomorrow
I'm leaving by plane / leaving (by other transport) tomorrow.

Помогите мне, пожалуйста, заполнить декларацию!
pamagityе mnye pazhalsta zapawlnit^s dyiklaratseeyoo
help-[!]-[formal/plural] to-me³ please to-fill-out declaration⁴
Can you please help me fill out the declaration?

сто пятьдесят три **153**

Customs

контроль	*kantrawl^{yi}*	control, inspection
таможня	*tamawzhnya*	customs
таможенная декларация	*tamawzhennaya dyiklaratseeya*	customs declaration
таможенный контроль	*tamawzhenneey kantrawl^{yi}*	customs inspection
таможенник	*tamawzhennik*	customs officer
пошлина	*pawshlina*	duty, tax
паспорт	*paspart*	passport
паспортный контроль	*paspartneey kantrawl^{yi}*	passport control
чемодан	*chyimadan*	suitcase
сумка	*soomka*	travel bag

Это подарки / личные вещи!
eta padarki / lichneeye vyeshchi
that gifts / personal things
Those are gifts / personal items!

Я протестую!
ya pratyistooyoo
I protest!

Police

Вызовите милицию!
vweezavitye militseeyoo
call-out-[!] police⁴
Call the police!

Где поблизости милиция?
gdye pablizasti militseeya
where-[!] nearby police
Where is the nearest police station?

На меня напали!
na myinya napali
on me⁴ they-attacked
I've been mugged!

Меня обокрали!
myinya abakrali
me⁴ they-robbed
I've been robbed!

Я потерял/потеряла свои документы.
ya patiyryal/patiyryala svai dakoomyentee
I lost-[m./f.] my-own documents
I've lost my documents.

TAKING PHOTOGRAPHS

батарейки	*bataryeyki*	batteries
аккумулятор	*akoomoolyatar*	battery pack
чёрно-белый	*chawrna-byeleey*	black and white
фотоаппарат	*fataaparat*	camera
адаптер	*adapter*	charger
цветной	*tsvyitnoy*	color
проявлять	*prayivlyatˢ*	develop (to ~)
проявка	*prayafka*	developing
цифровой фотоаппарат	*tseefravoy fataaparat*	digital camera
одноразовый фотоаппарат	*adnarazaveey fataaparat*	disposable camera
плёнка	*plyawnka*	film
снимать на камеру	*snimatˢ na kamyiroo*	film (to ~)
вспышка	*fspeeshka*	flash
объектив	*abᵒyektif*	lens
карта памяти	*karta pamyiti*	memory card
фотография	*fatagrafiya*	photograph, photography
фотографировать	*fatagrafiravatˢ*	photograph (to ~)
отпечаток	*atpyichatak*	print
печать	*pyichatˢ*	print (to ~)

| записать фото на CD | zapisatᵉ fawta na si-di | save photos to a CD (to ~) |
| плёнка для слайдов | plyawnka dlya slaydaf | slide film |

Можно здесь фотографировать?
mawzhna zdyesʸⁱ fatagrafiravatᵉ
it-is-possible here to-photograph
Is it all right to take photos here?

Сколько времени длится тиражирование CD?
skawlʸⁱka vryemini dlitsa tirazheevaniye si-di
how-much time² lasts-self development CD
How long does it take to burn [photos to] a CD?

SMOKING / NO SMOKING?

Можно здесь курить?
mawzhna zdyesʸⁱ kooritᵉ
it-is-possible here to-smoke
Is it all right to smoke here?

Курить запрещено!
kooritᵉ zapryishchyinaw
to-smoke forbidden
Smoking is prohibited!

У вас есть зажигалка?
oo vas yestᵉ zazheegalka
in-the-possession of-you²-[formal/plural] there-is lighter
Do you have a light?

сигареты	sigaryetee	cigarettes
папиросы	papirawsee	cigarettes with cardboard filter
сигареты с фильтром	sigaryetee s-filʸⁱtram	filter cigarettes
зажигалка	zazheegalka	lighter

спички (f. pl.)	spichki	matches
трубка	troopka	pipe
табак	tabak	tobacco
сигареты без фильтра	sigaryetee bis-fil'tra	unfiltered cigarettes

HEALTH

Medical services are mostly provided by health centers and hospitals in Russia. Very few doctors work in private practice.

регистрация	ryigistratseeya	admissions office
часы приёма	chisee priyawma	consultation hours
врач	vrach	doctor
поликлиника	paliklinika	health center
больница	bal'nitsa	hospital
приёмная	priyawmnaya	waiting room

На помощь!
na pawmashch'
Help!

Скорее, врача!
skaryeye vracha
Quick! A doctor!

Осторожнее!
astarawzhnyiye
Careful!

Вызовите врача / скорую помощь!
vweezavitye vracha / skawrooyoo pawmashch'
call-out-[!] doctor[4] / fast[4] help[4]
Call a doctor / an ambulance!

At the Doctor's

Я болен/больна.
ya bawlyin/bal'na
I sick-[m./f.]
I'm sick.

На что жалуетесь?
na shtaw zhalooyityis'
on what you-complain-self-[formal/plural]
What's the matter?

Я БОЛЕН.
(I'm sick.)

У меня болит...	oo myinya balit	I have pain in my...
спина	spina	back
живот	zheevawt	belly
грудная клетка	groodnaya klyetka	chest / thorax
ухо	ookha	ear
нога	naga	foot / leg
рука	rooka	hand / arm
голова	galava	head
сердце	syertse	heart
почки	pawchki	kidneys
плечо	plyichaw	shoulder
желудок	zheloodak	stomach
горло	gawrla	throat

У меня...	oo myinya	I have...
аллергия	alyirgiya	allergy (an ~)
кашель (m.)	kasheel^{yi}	cough (a ~)
понос	panaws	diarrhea
жар	zhar	fever (a ~)
грипп	grip	flu (the ~)

головная боль (f.)	galavnaya bawl[yi]	headache (a ~)
сердечные боли	syirdyechneeye bawli	heart pain
воспаление	vaspalyeniye	inflammation (an ~)
тошнота	tashnata	nausea
боли (pl.)	bawli	pain
температура	tyimpyiratoora	temperature (a ~)

У меня здесь болит!
oo myinya zdyes[yi] balit
in-the-possession of-me² here hurts
It hurts here!

У меня одноразовые шприцы.
oo myinya adnarazavweeye shpritsee
in-the-possession of-me² one-time syringes
I have disposable syringes.

Я болен/больна диабетом.
ya bawlyin/bal[yi]na diabyetam
I sick-[m./f.] with-diabetes⁵
I have diabetes / I am diabetic.

Мне нужна справка для моей страховки.
mnye noozhna sprafka dlya mayey strakhawfki
to-me³ is-necessary-[f.] certificate for my² insurance²
I need a certificate for my insurance.

At the Dentist's

зубной врач	zoobnoy vrach	dentist
пломба	plawmba	filling
зуб	zoop	tooth

Запломбируйте, не удаляйте, пожалуйста!
zaplambirooytye nyi oodalyaytye pazhalsta
fill-[!] not remove-[!] please
Can you give me a filling please? Don't pull the tooth!

At the Pharmacy

We advise you to take an adequate supply of your usual medicines to Russia with you. It's also a good idea to pack a first aid kit.

бинт	*bint*	bandage
вата	*v<u>a</u>ta*	cotton wool
подгузники	*padg<u>oo</u>zniki*	diapers / nappies
капли (pl.)	*k<u>a</u>pli*	drops
наружное	*nar<u>oo</u>zhnaye*	external use
для детей	*dlya dyity<u>e</u>y*	for children
мазь	*mas*[yi]	ointment
аптека	*apty<u>e</u>ka*	pharmacy
средство	*sry<u>e</u>tstva*	remedy, drug
гигиенические прокладки	*gigiyinichyiskiye prakl<u>a</u>tki*	sanitary napkins
снотворное средство	*snatv<u>aw</u>rnaye sry<u>e</u>tstva*	sleeping pill
пластырь (m.)	*plast<u>ee</u>r*[yi]	sticking plaster
свечка	*svy<u>i</u>chka*	suppository
таблетка	*tably<u>e</u>tka*	tablet
принимать	*prinim<u>a</u>t*[s]	take (to ~)
~ внутрь	*vn<u>oo</u>tr*[yi]	~ orally
градусник, термометр	*gr<u>a</u>doosnik, tyirm<u>aw</u>myitr*	thermometer

Дайте мне что-нибудь от головной боли/поноса.
d<u>ay</u>tye mnye sht<u>aw</u>-nibo<u>o</u>t[s] at galavn<u>o</u>y b<u>aw</u>li/pan<u>aw</u>sa
give-[!] to-me³ something from head ache²/diarrhea²
Can you give me something for a headache/diarrhea, please?

Как принимать лекарство?
kak prinimat͡ɛ lyikarstva
how to-take medicine
How should I take this medicine?

The Assimil method

The "With Ease" Series

To help you learn foreign languages with ease and pleasure, Assimil has developed an exclusive, highly effective Method.

Intuitive Assimilation®

The Assimil Method is based on a simple principle: applying the same natural process that enabled you to learn your mother tongue. Through lively dialogues, simple explanations and easy exercises, Assimil gradually guides you from your first words to full conversational fluency.

In the first part of the method (Passive Phase), the learning process is passive – you simply "absorb" the language.

At midpoint, you start the Active Phase, where you form your own sentences.

Within a few months – whatever the language you're learning, you'll be able to speak effortlessly and without hesitating, in other words, naturally.

The Assimil method

Our Method is available in English for the languages below.

Beginner Level:
Arabic With Ease
Chinese With Ease
Dutch With Ease
New French With Ease
German With Ease
Hungarian With Ease
Italian With Ease
Japanese With Ease
Spanish With Ease

Advanced Level:
Using French
Business French

Ask for ASSIMIL at your bookstore!

Assimil Method books
are available with recordings on CD or MP3.
In selected languages, the Method is available in two steps: Beginner and Advanced.

GLOSSARY

The introduction contains a list of the abbreviations used in this book.

Unless otherwise indicated, verbs are shown in the imperfective aspect and belong to Group 1 (see **Verbs, The present tense**). In the English-Russian glossary, the two aspects (imperfective and perfective) of verbs are given one after the other, separated by a slash.

Nouns are given in the singular. For the most common nouns, the plural form is given in brackets if it is irregular.

Adjectives are given in the masculine singular nominative.

RUSSIAN – ENGLISH

А

а	but
авария (f.)	accident
австралиец (m.)	Australian (man)
австралийка (f.)	Australian (woman)
австралийский	Australian (adj.)
Австралия (f.)	Australia
автобус (m.)	bus
автомагистраль (f.)	highway, motorway
автомастерская (f.)	garage (auto repairs)
автомашина (f.)	car (automobile)
автостоянка (f.)	parking space
администрация (f.)	administration
адрес (m.)	address
алкоголь (m.)	alcohol
Америка (f.)	America
американец (m.)	American (man)
американка (f.)	American (woman)
американский	American (adj.)
английский	English (adj.)
англичанин (m.)	English (man)
англичанка (f.)	English (woman)
Англия (f.)	England
аптека (f.)	pharmacy
аэропорт (m.)	airport

Б

багаж (m.)	luggage
балет (m.)	ballet
бандероль (f.)	small parcel
банк (m.)	bank
батарейка (f.)	battery
башня (f.)	tower
бедный	poor
бежать III (unidir.) / бегать (multidir.)	to run
без...[2]	without

бельё (n.)	sheets
бензин (m.)	gasoline, petrol
бензопункт (m.)	service station
беременная	pregnant
бесплатный	free of charge
билет (m.)	ticket
бинт (m.)	bandage
бить II	to beat
благодаря...[3]	thanks to
бланк (m.)	form
близко (adv.)	near, close
бог (m.)	God
богатый	rich
болезнь (f.)	sickness
болен	sick
болит (это ~) (3rd pers. sg.)	it hurts
боль (f.)	pain
больной	sick
больше (чем)	more (than)
большой	big
бояться III	to fear, to be afraid of
брат (m.) (и сестра (f.))	brother (and sister)
брать II / взять II (perf.)	to take (umbrella, taxi, etc.)
брать напрокат II	to rent (as the renter)
бродить III	to wander
бронировать / забронировать (perf.)	to reserve, to book
будить III / разбудить III (perf.)	to wake (someone) up
будьте здоровы!	bless you!
буква (f.)	letter (of alphabet)
булочка (f.)	bun, bread roll
бумага (f.)	paper
бутылка (f.)	bottle
быстро!	quick!
быть	to be
бюро (=, n.)	office, bureau
бюро путешествий (n.)	travel agency

В

в...[4]	to, into, on, in
в...[6]	at, in
вагон (m.)	car (of train)
важный	important
валюта (f.)	currency
ванная (f.)	bathroom
варить III	to cook (to heat food)
вата (f.)	cotton wool
вдруг	suddenly
вежливый	polite
везде	everywhere
велосипед (m.)	bicycle
верить III	to believe
вес (m.)	weight
весёлый	happy (jolly, merry)
весна (f.)	spring
ветер (m.)	wind
вечер (m.) (pl. вечера)	evening
взлом (m.)	burglary
взять II (perf.) машину на буксир	to tow a car
видеть III	to see
видеться III	to see each other
вилка (f.)	fork
вина (f.)	fault
виновный	at fault, in the wrong
визит (m.)	visit (official)
вкусный	tasty, delicious
владелец (m.)	owner
влюблённый	in love
вместе	together
вместо...[2]	instead of
внизу	on the bottom, underneath

внутри	inside
во время	during
вовремя	in time
вода (f.)	water
воздух (m.)	air
возможно	(it is) possible
возраст (m.)	age
вокзал (m.)	railway station
восток (m.)	east
врач (m.)	doctor
время (n.)	time
время года (n.)	season
всё (n.)	all
всегда	always
вспоминать	to remember
вставать	to get up
встреча (f.)	meeting
встречать	to meet
встречаться	to meet (each other)
вход (m.)	entrance
входить III	to enter, to go in
вчера	yesterday
вывоз (m.)	export
выезд (m.)	departure
выигрывать	to win
выражать	to express
высокий	high, tall
выставка (f.)	exhibition
выход (m.)	exit
выходить III / выйти II (perf.)	to exit, to leave

Г

газ (m.)	gas
газета (f.)	newspaper
где	where
гигиена (f.)	hygiene
гладить III	to iron
глубокий	deep
глупый	stupid
гнилой	rotten
говорить III / сказать (perf.)	to speak, to say
год (m.)	year
голодный	hungry
голос (m.) (pl. голоса)	voice
голый	naked
гора (f.)	mountain
гореть III	to burn
город (pl. города) (m.)	city, town
горький	bitter
гостеприимство (n.)	hospitality
гостиница (f.)	hotel
гость (m.)	guest
готов!	ready!
готовить III	to prepare, to cook
гражданин (m.)	citizen (man)
гражданка (f.)	citizen (woman)
гражданство (n.)	citizenship
грамм (m.)	gram
граница (f.)	border
грипп (m.)	flu
гроза (f.)	storm
громкий	loud
грубый	rude, crude
группа (f.)	group
грязный	dirty

Д

да	yes
давать II / дать (perf.)	to give
далеко	far
дверь (f.)	door
дворец (m.)	palace
девочка (f.)	girl (little girl)
девушка (f.)	girl (young woman)
действительный	real, genuine
делать / сделать (perf.)	to do, to make
делать укол	to give an injection

день *(m.)*	day
день рождения *(m.)*	birthday
деньги *(pl. only)*	money
деревня *(f.)*	village, countryside
дерево *(n.)*	wood
держать в руке	to hold in your hand
дети *(irreg. pl.)*	children
дёшево	cheap
джинсы *(pl. only)*	jeans
дискотека *(f.)*	disco
для...²	for (a purpose/category)
до...²	until
до обеда	before lunchtime
довольно!	that's enough!
договариваться / договориться III	to agree (reach an agreement)
дождь *(m.)*	rain
документ *(m.)*	document
документы *(pl.)*	documents
долго *(adv.)*	long (for a long time)
долина *(f.)*	valley
доллар *(m.)*	dollar
дом *(m.) (pl.* дома*)*	house, home
дорога *(f.)*	road
дорогой	expensive, dear
дорожная карта *(f.)*	road map
достаточно! *(adv.)*	that's enough!
достопримечательность *(f.)*	tourist sight
друг *(m.) (pl.* друзья*)*	(boy)friend
другой	other
дружба *(f.)*	friendship
думать	to think
дыра *(f.)*	hole

Е / Ё

евро (=, *m.*)	euro
еда *(f.)*	food
ежегодный	annual
ежедневный	everyday *(adj.)*
если	if
есть	to eat
есть *(impers.)*	there is
ехать *(unidir.)* / ездить III *(multidir.)*	to go (by vehicle)
ещё	again, still

Ж

жаловаться	to complain
жар *(m.)*	fever
ждать II	to wait for
желать	to wish
жена *(f.) (pl.* жёны*)*	wife
женщина *(f.)*	woman
живот *(m.)*	belly
животное *(n.)*	animal
жизнь *(f.)*	life
житель *(m.)*	resident
жить II	to live

З

за...⁴	for (in exchange for / for a reason)
за...⁴...⁵	behind
заблуждаться	to get lost
забывать / забыть *(perf.)*	to forget
завтра	tomorrow
завтрак *(m.)*	breakfast
завтракать	to have breakfast
заграница	abroad
заезжать за...⁵	to pick (someone) up
заказ *(m.)*	order
заказывать / заказать *(perf.)*	to order
закон *(m.)*	law
закрывать / закрыть *(perf.)*	to close
замок *(m.)*	castle
заниматься...⁵	to be occupied with, to do

запад (m.)	west
запасная часть (f.)	spare part
заполнить	to fill out (a form)
запоминать	to keep in mind
зарабатывать	to earn
запрещён, запрещена (f.), -но (m.), -ны (pl.)	forbidden
заходить III / зайти II (perf.)	to drop in on someone
звонить III / позвонить III (по телефону)	to telephone
здание (n.)	building
здоровье (n.)	health
здоровый	healthy
земля (f.)	earth, land
зима (f.)	winter
знакомиться III / познакомиться III (perf.)	to make someone's acquaintance, to meet someone (for the first time)
знаменитый	famous
знать	to know
золото (n.)	gold
зоопарк (m.)	zoo
зубная паста (f.)	toothpaste
зубной врач (m.)	dentist

И

и	and
иголка (f.)	needle
игрушка (f.)	toy
идти II (unidir.) / ходить III (multidir.)	to go (on foot)
из,[2]	from (a place)
известие (n. sg.)	news
известный	famous
извините!	sorry! (excuse me!)
извиниться III	apologize
или	or
или... или...	either... or...
иметь	to have
импорт (m.)	import
имя (n.) (pl. имена)	(first) name
иногда	sometimes
иностранец (m.)	foreigner (man)
иностранка (f.)	foreigner (woman)
интересный	interesting
интересовать	to interest
интересоваться	to take an interest in
информация (f.)	information
ирландец (m.)	Irish (man)
Ирландия (f.)	Ireland
ирландка (f.)	Irish (woman)
ирландский	Irish (adj.)
искать	to look for
искусство (n.)	art
история (f.)	history

К

к...[3]	to (someone's house)
каждый	every
каждый раз	every time
как	how
камень (m.)	stone
Канада (f.)	Canada
канадец (m.)	Canadian (man)
канадка (f.)	Canadian (woman)
канадский (adj.)	Canadian
каникулы (pl. only)	vacation
карандаш (m.)	pencil
карта Москвы (f.)	map of Moscow
картина (f.)	picture, painting (art)
касса (f.)	cash desk, ticket booth
качество (n.)	quality
квартира (f.)	apartment
кино (=, n.)	cinema (movie theater)

кинотеатр (m.)	cinema (movie theater)
класть II / положить III (perf.)	to put (something upright)
ключ (m.)	key
книга (f.)	book
когда	when
колесо (n.) (pl. колёса)	wheel
количество (n.)	quantity
комната (f.)	room
коммутатор (m.)	(telephone) operator
комплект (m.)	set
конец (m.)	end
конечно!	of course!
консульство (n.)	consulate
концерт (m.)	concert
коридор (m.)	corridor
короткий	short
кофе (m.)	coffee
кража (f.)	theft, robbery
красивый	beautiful
крепкий	strong (person, wine, etc.)
кричать III	to yell
кровать (f.)	bed
кроме	except
кто-нибудь	someone
куда	to where
купаться	to swim (to go bathing)
купе (n.)	compartment
курить III	to smoke
кухня (f.)	kitchen, cooking
кушайте!	eat! (polite)
кушанье (n.)	food

Л

лампа (f.)	lamp
лёгкий	light, easy
лёд (m.)	ice
лежать III	to lie down
лекарство (n.)	medicine
ленивый	lazy
лес (m.) (pl. леса)	forest
лестница (f.)	staircase
летать (unidir.) / лететь III (multidir.)	to fly
лето (n.)	summer
лечить III	to cure
ли	if (interrogative particle)
лодка (f.)	boat
ложка (f.)	spoon
лучше всего	the best thing
лучше чем	better than
лучший	better
льгота (f.)	advantage, benefit
любить III	to love, to like
любовь (f.) (pl. любви)	love
любопытно	strange, curious
люди (pl. only)	people

М

магазин (m.)	shop
маленький	small
мало...[2]	few, not many
мальчик (m.)	boy
масло (n.)	butter, oil
мастерская (f.)	workshop
материал (m.)	material
мать (f.) (pl. матери)	mother
машина (f.)	car (automobile)
медленный	slow
между...[5]	between
международный	international
мелочь (f.)	small change
меню (n.)	menu
менять	to change
меняться	to exchange
мёрзнуть	to be cold
мёртвый	dead
местность (f.)	place, locality

место (n.)	place, seat (on transport, in a theatre)	надеяться	to hope
		надо (impers.)	(it is) necessary
		назад	behind
месяц (m.)	month	назад (тому ~)	ago
мешать	to bother	наилучший	best
милиционер (m.)	policeman	наконец	finally
милиция (f.)	police	налево	(on the) left
минута (f.)	minute	наличные (pl. only)	cash
много	many		
мода (f.)	fashion	наложенным платежом	cash on delivery
может быть	maybe		
можно (impers.)	(it is) possible, allowed	напиток (m.)	drink
		направо	(on the) right
мокрый	wet	напрокат	for rent
молодой	young	напротив!	on the contrary!
моложе чем	younger than	народ (m.)	(the) people
море (n.)	sea	настоящий	real
мороженое (n.) (collective, no pl.)	ice cream	находится	is located
		находить III / найти II (perf.)	to find
мост (m.)	bridge		
мотор (m.)	engine	находиться III	to be located
моторная лодка (f.)	motorboat	национальность (f.)	nationality, ethnic group
моторное масло (n.)	engine oil	начало (n.)	start
		начинать / начать II (perf.)	to start
мотоцикл (m.)	motorcycle		
мочь / смочь (perf.)	can	не	not
		не работает	is not working
муж (m.) (pl. мужья)	husband	небо (n.)	sky
		невиновный	innocent (not guilty)
мужчина (m.)	man		
музей (m.)	museum	недалеко	not far
музыка (f.)	music	неделя (f.)	week
мыло (n.)	soap	недорого	inexpensive
мыть	to wash	незнакомый	unknown
мясо (n.)	meat	немного	a little
Н		немного...[2]	a little (of something)
на...[4]	to, into, on, onto, for, in	ненужный	unnecessary
		неправильно!	that's wrong!
на...[6]	at, in, on	несколько	some, a few
наверх	up	нет	no
наверху	on the top, above	нет...[2]	there is no
		ни... ни	neither... nor

сто семьдесят один **171**

низкий	low
никогда	never
никто	no one
ничто	nothing
но	but
Новая Зеландия (f.)	New Zealand
новозеландец (m.)	New Zealander (man)
новозеландка (f.)	New Zealander (woman)
новозеландский	New Zealand (adj.)
новый	new
нога (f.)	leg, foot
нож (m.)	knife
ножницы (pl. only)	scissors
номер (m.) (pl. номера)	number, hotel room
нормальный	normal
носить III	to carry, to bring, to wear
ночевать / переночевать (perf.)	to spend the night
ночь (f.)	night
нравиться III / понравиться III (perf.)	to please, (to like)
нужно (impers.)	to need

О

о...[6]	about
обед (m.)	lunch
обедать	to have lunch
обижать	to offend
облако (n.) (pl. облака)	cloud
обманывать	to cheat, to swindle
обратно	back (adv.)
обращаться (к...[3])	to turn to, to approach (someone)
обслуживание (n.)	service
обувь (f. sg.)	shoes
обучать	to teach
общество (n.)	society
общежитие (n.)	dormitory, hostel
объезд (m.)	detour
объяснять	to explain
обычай (m.)	habit, custom
обычно	usually
обязательный	essential
овощи (m. pl.)	vegetables
огонь (m.)	fire
одалживать	to lend
одежда (f. sg.)	a piece of clothing, clothes
один / одна (f.)	one, a, a single
озеро (n.) (pl. озёра)	lake
оканчивать	to finish
окно (n.)	window
около...[2]	around
окольный путь (m.)	detour
окружение (n.)	environment
опаздывать / опоздать (perf.)	to be late
опасный	dangerous
опять	again
организовать	to organize
осень (f.)	fall, autumn
осматривать / осмотреть III (perf.)	to visit (a place)
оставаться II / остаться (perf.)	to stay
останавливать / остановить III (perf.)	to stop (someone or something)
остановка (f.)	stop, station (transport)
остров (m.) (pl. острова)	island
острый	sharp, spicy
от...[2]	from (a person or a person's place)

ответ (m.)	answer	переводчица (f.)	translator (woman)
ответственность (f.)	responsibility	перед...⁵	before
отвечать	to answer	перед обедом	before lunchtime
отдавать II / отдать (perf.)	to give back	переодеваться	to change (clothes)
отдыхать	to rest, to relax	переписываться	to correspond (with someone)
отец (m.)	father	перерыв (m.)	break, pause
открывать / открыть (perf.)	to open	переселяться	to move house
открытка (f.)	postcard	переставать II	to stop (doing something)
отличный	excellent	переулок (m.)	lane
отпуск (m.) (pl. отпуска)	vacation (leave from work)	персона (f.)	person
отъезд (m.)	departure	песня (f.)	song
официант (m.)	waiter	петь	to sing
официантка (f.)	waitress	печальный	sad
охотиться III	to hunt	пешком	on foot
охотно!	with pleasure!	пиво (n.)	beer
очень	very	пирог (m.)	pie
очки (pl. only)	glasses	писать / написать (perf.)	to write
ошибаться	to make a mistake	письмо (n.)	letter (missive)
ошибка (f.)	mistake	пить II	to drink
П		плавать	to swim
падать	to fall	плакать	to cry
пакет (m.)	packet	план (m.)	plan
палатка (f.)	tent	плата за проезд (f.)	price for the journey
палец (m.) (pl. пальцы)	finger	платить III / заплатить III (perf.)	to pay
папироса (f.)	short, unfiltered cigarette		
пара (f.)	a pair	платформа (f.)	platform
парк (m.)	park	плацкарта (f.)	reservation
паром (m.)	ferry	плёнка (f.)	film
паспорт (m.) (pl. паспорта)	passport	плохой	bad
пациент (m.)	patient (medical)	плохо (adv.)	bad, badly
пейзаж (m.)	landscape, scenery	площадь (f.)	square (in city)
		по-английски	in English
перевод (m.)	bank transfer	повторять / повторить III (perf.)	to repeat
переводить III / перевести II (perf.)	to translate		
переводчик (m.)	translator (man)	погода (f.)	weather

под...⁴...⁵	under
подкладка (f.)	sanitary napkin
подождать II	wait for (to ~)
подписывать / подписать (perf.)	to sign
подруга (f.)	(girl)friend
поезд (m.) (pl. поезда)	train
поездка (f.)	journey
пожалуйста	please
поздно	(it's) late, too late
поздравлять	to congratulate
пока!	bye!
показывать / показать (perf.)	to show
покупать / купить III (perf.)	to buy
поле (n.)	field
политика (f. sg.)	politics, policy
половина (f.)	half
положение (n.)	position (geographical)
полотенце (n.)	towel
получать / получить III (perf.)	to receive
пользоваться	to use
полный	full
поменять (perf.)	to exchange (things)
понимать / понять II (perf.)	to understand
понос (m.)	diarrhea
порт (m.)	port, harbor
по-русски	in Russian
посещать / посетить III (perf.)	to visit (a place)
посещение (n.)	visit
после...²	after
после обеда	after lunch, in the afternoon
посольство (n.)	embassy
поставить машину III (perf.)	to park the car
постель (f.)	bed
посылать	to send
потеть	to perspire
потому что	because
поцелуй (m.)	kiss
почта (f.)	post office
(почтовая марка) (f.)	(postage) stamp
пошлина (f.)	tax, duty
правда (f.)	truth
правильный	right (correct)
право (n.)	right (legal right)
праздник (m.)	holiday, feast day
праздновать	to celebrate
прачечная (f.)	laundry (place)
пребывание (n.)	stay
предлагать	to propose
предприятие (n.)	enterprise, company
представлять / представить III (perf.)	to present
прежде чем	earlier than
презерватив (m.)	condom
прекрасный	lovely
преступление (n.)	crime
прибывать / прибыть (perf.)	to arrive
прибытие (n.)	arrival
привет!	hi!
привет (m.)	greetings
приветливый	welcoming
приветствовать	to greet
прививать	to vaccinate
прививка (f.)	vaccination
приглашать	to invite
приглашение (n.)	invitation
приготавливать / приготовить III (perf.)	to prepare
прийти II (perf.)	to come
прилежный	hard-working
принимать	to take (shower, medicine, decision, etc.); to accept

принимать душ	to take a shower
приносить III / принести II (perf.)	to bring
природа (f.)	nature
приятно!	nice to meet you!
проблема (f.)	problem
пробовать	to try, to taste
проверять	to check
проводник (m.)	conductor
провожать	to accompany
программа (f.)	program
прогуливаться	to stroll
прогулка (f.)	stroll
продавать II	to sell
продовольствие (n.)	food
произношение (n.)	pronunciation
промышленность (f.)	industry
прописывать	to register (a document)
проспект (m.)	avenue
простой	simple
просто	simply
простуда (f.)	cold (sickness)
простужен	to have a cold
простыня (f.)	sheet
просьба (f.)	request
против...[2]	against
профессия (f.)	occupation, profession
прохладный	cool (temperature)
прощаться	to say goodbye
птица (f.)	bird, poultry
пустой	empty
путешествовать	to travel
пьяный	drunk

Р

работа (f.)	work
работать	to work
рад	glad
радио (=, n.)	radio
раз (один ~)	once
развлекаться	to enjoy oneself
разговаривать	to talk, to chat
разговор (m.)	conversation
раздевать	to undress
разрешать	to permit
разрешение (n.)	permission
рана (f.)	wound, injury
рано (adv.)	early
раньше	earlier, previously
расписание (n.)	timetable
рассказ (m.)	story
рассказывать / рассказать (perf.)	to tell (a story)
ребёнок (m.)	child
регистрировать	to register
регулярный	regular
редкий	rare
река (f.)	river
ремонт (m.)	repair, renovation
ремонтировать	to repair, to renovate
решать	to decide
родители (pl. only)	parents
Россия (f.)	Russia
Российская Федерация (f.)	Russian Federation
рубль (m.)	ruble
рука (f.)	arm, hand
русская (f.)	Russian (woman)
русский (m.)	Russian (man)
русский	Russian (adj.)
рыба (f.)	fish
рынок (m.)	market

С

с...[5]	with
с тех пор	since then
садиться III / сесть (perf.)	to sit down
садиться III	to board (transport)
салфетка (f.)	napkin
самолёт (m.)	plane

свадьба (f.)	wedding
свежий	fresh
свет (m.)	light (noun)
свободный	free, vacant
сворачивать / свернуть II (perf.)	to turn
сдавать внаём II	to rent out
север (m.)	north
сейчас	now
секунда (f.)	second (noun)
сельское хозяйство (n.)	agriculture
серебро (n.)	silver
сестра (f.) (pl. сёстры)	sister
сигарета (f.)	cigarette
сидеть III	to be seated
сидит	(it) suits (clothes)
сильный	strong (person, will, smell, etc.)
скамья (f.)	bench
скорая помощь (f.)	ambulance
скоро	soon
скучный	boring
сладкий	sweet
слева (adv.)	left
слишком (много)	too many
словарь (m.)	dictionary
слово (n.)	word
сложный	complicated, hard
служащий (m.)	office worker, employee
слышать / услышать III (perf.)	to hear
смерть (f.)	death
смеяться II	to laugh
смотреть III	to watch, to look
снаружи	on the outside
снег (m.) (pl. снега)	snow
согласен/ согласна/-о/-ни (m./f./n./pl.)	in agreement
солнце (n.)	sun
собственность (f.)	property
советовать	to recommend
совсем	completely
совсем нет	absolutely not
сообщать / сообщить III (perf.)	to communicate, to inform
сосуд (m.)	container
спальня (f.)	bedroom
спасибо	thank you
спать III	to sleep
СПИД (m.)	AIDS
спичка (f.)	match (to light)
спорить III	to argue, to bet
спорт (m.)	sport
справа	right
справка (f.)	information
справляться	to find out
справочное бюро (n.)	information desk
спрашивать / спросить III (perf.)	to ask
срочный	urgent
срочно (adv.)	urgently
ставить III / поставить III (perf.)	to put (something flat)
стакан (m.)	glass (for drinking)
старый	old
стекло (n.) (pl. стёкла)	glass (material)
стена (f.)	wall
стоит (это ~)	it costs
стоять III	to stand
страна (f.)	country
страх (m.)	fear, fright
страховка (f.)	insurance
стрелять	to shoot
строить III / построить III (perf.)	to build
студент (m.)	(male) student
студентка (f.)	(female) student

судно (n.) (pl. суда)	ship
сумма (f.)	sum, total
сумка (f.)	bag
суп (m.)	soup
супруги (pl.)	husband and wife (married couple)
сухой	dry
счастливый	happy (fulfilled)
счастье (n.)	happiness
счёт (m.) (pl. счета)	check, bill
считать	to count
сын (m.) (pl. сыновья)	son
сырой	humid, damp

Т

табак (m.)	tobacco
таблетка (f.)	tablet, pill
так	so, therefore
такси (=, n.)	taxi
таможня (f.)	customs
танцевать	to dance
твёрдый	hard (not soft)
те (pl.)	those
театр (m.)	theater
телевизор (m.)	television
телеграмма (f.)	telegram
телефон (m.)	telephone
тёмный	dark
теперь	now
тёплый	warm
территория (f.)	territory
терять / потерять (perf.)	to lose
тесный	tight
ткань (f.)	fabric
товар (m.)	merchandise
тоже	also
только	only
тонкий	thin
торговля (f.)	trade
торопиться III	to hurry
тот	that one
точный	exact
точно	exactly
традиция (f.)	tradition
трамвай (m.)	tram
трос (m.)	rope
труд (m.)	work, labor
трудный	difficult
туалет (m.)	toilet
туалетная бумага (f.)	toilet paper
туда	to there
турист (m.)	(male) tourist
туристка (f.)	(female) tourist

У

у...[2]	at the house of, in one's possession
убивать	to kill
уведомлять	to inform
уже	already
ужин (m.)	dinner
ужинать / поужинать (perf.)	to have dinner
уезжать / уехать (unidir.)	to leave (by vehicle)
укол (m.)	injection
украшение (n.)	decoration
улетать / улететь III (perf.)	to leave (by plane)
улица (f.)	street
улыбаться	to smile
уметь	to be able to
умный	clever
умирать	to die
универмаг (m.)	department store
университет (m.)	university
успех (m.)	success
усталый	tired
утро (n.)	morning

утром	in the morning
утюг (m.)	iron (for clothes)
ученик (m.)	(boy) pupil
ученица (f.)	(girl) pupil
учиться III	to learn
уютный	cosy

Ф

фамилия (f.)	surname
фильм (m.)	film
флирт (m.)	flirtation
флиртировать	to flirt
фото (=, n.)	photo
фотоаппарат (m.)	camera
фотографировать / сфотографировать (perf.)	to photograph
фрукт (m.)	fruit
фунт (m.)	pound (sterling)

Х

хлеб (m.)	bread
хозяин (m.)	host, owner, landlord
хозяйка (f.)	hostess, owner, landlady
холодный	cold
холостой (m.)	bachelor
хороший (adj.)	good
хорошо (adv.)	well, good
хотеть	to want

Ц

цвет (m.) (pl. цвета)	color
цветок (m.) (pl. цветы)	flower
целовать	to kiss
цена (f.)	price
центр (m.)	center
церковь (f.)	church

Ч

чаевые (pl. only)	tip
чай (m.)	tea
час (m.)	hour, time
частный	private
часто	often
часть (в)...[2]	part (of)
часы (pl. only)	watch (timepiece)
чек (m.)	cheque (check)
человек (m.)	man, person
чем	than
через...[4]	through
читать / прочитать (perf.)	to read
чтобы	in order to
чувство (n.)	feeling
чувствовать	to feel
чужой	other (belonging to another)

Ш

шотландец (m.)	Scot (man)
Шотландия (f.)	Scotland
шотландка (f.)	Scot (woman)
шотландский	Scottish (adj.)
шина (f.)	tire (of car)
широкий	wide
школа (f.)	school
шприц (m.)	syringe
штраф (m.)	fine (penalty)
штука (f.)	item

Э

экономить III	to save money
экскурсия (f.)	excursion, tour
экспорт (m.)	export
это (n.)	that, it (pronoun) (e.g. it's hot)
этот/эта/это (m./f./n.)	that (demonstrative article) (e.g. that boy)

Ю

юг *(m.)* south

Я

яд *(m.)* poison
ядовитая змея *(f.)* venomous snake

язык *(m.)* language
(*pl.* **языки**)

ENGLISH – RUSSIAN

A

a (a single)	один / одна (f.)
able (to be ~ to)	уметь
about	о...[6]
above	наверху
abroad	заграница
absolutely not	совсем нет
accept (to ~)	принимать
accident	авария (f.)
accompany (to ~)	провожать
address	адрес (m.)
administration	администрация (f.)
advantage	льгота (f.)
afraid (to be ~ of)	бояться III
after	после...[2]
after lunch	после обеда
afternoon (in the ~)	после обеда
again	опять
again (still)	ещё
against	против...[2]
age	возраст (m.)
ago	назад, тому назад
agree (to ~) (share the same opinion)	согласен/ согласна/-о/-ни (m./f./n./pl.)
agree (to ~) (reach an agreement)	договариваться / договориться III
agriculture	сельское хозяйство (n.)
AIDS	СПИД (m.)
air	воздух (m.)
airport	аэропорт (m.)
alcohol	алкоголь (m.)
all	всё (n.)
already	уже
also	тоже
always	всегда
ambulance	скорая помощь (f.)
America	Америка (f.)
American (man)	американец (m.)
American (woman)	американка (f.)
American (adj.)	американский
and	и
animal	животное (n.)
annual	ежегодный
answer	ответ (m.)
answer (to ~)	отвечать
apartment	квартира (f.)
apologize (to ~)	извиниться III
approach (to ~) (someone)	обращаться (к...[3])
argue (to ~)	спорить III
arm	рука (f.)
around	около...[2]
arrival	прибытие (n.)
arrive (to ~)	прибывать / прибыть (perf.)
art	искусство (m.)
ask (to ~)	спрашивать / спросить III (perf.)
at	в...[6], на...[6]
at the house of	у...[2]
Australia	Австралия (f.)
Australian (man)	австралиец (m.)
Australian (woman)	австралийка (f.)
Australian (adj.)	австралийский
autumn	осень (f.)
avenue	проспект (m.)

B

bachelor	холостой (m.)
back	обратно (adv.)
bad	плохой
bad (badly)	плохо (adv.)
bag	сумка (f.)
ballet	балет (m.)
bandage	бинт (m.)
bank	банк (m.)
bank transfer	перевод (m.)

bathroom	ванная (f.)
battery	батарейка (f.)
be (to ~)	быть
beat (to ~)	бить II
beautiful	красивый
because	потому что
bed	кровать (f.), постель (f.)
bedroom	спальня (f.)
beer	пиво (n.)
before	перед...[5]
before lunchtime (in the morning)	перед обедом, до обеда
behind	за...[4]...[5]
behind (at the back)	назад
believe (to ~)	верить III
belly	живот (m.)
bench	скамья (f.)
benefit	льгота (f.)
best (the ~ thing)	лучше всего
best	наилучший
bet (to ~)	спорить III
better	лучший
better than	лучше чем
between	между...[5]
bicycle	велосипед (m.)
big	большой
bill (check)	счёт (m.) (pl. счета)
bird	птица (f.)
birthday	день (m.) рождения (m.)
bitter	горький
bless you!	будьте здоровы!
board (to ~) (transport)	садиться III
boat	лодка (f.)
book	книга (f.)
border	граница (f.)
boring	скучный
bother (to ~)	мешать
bottle	бутылка (f.)
bottom (on the ~)	внизу
boy	мальчик (m.)
bread	хлеб (m.)
break	перерыв (m.)
breakfast	завтрак (m.)
breakfast (to have ~)	завтракать
bridge	мост (m.)
bring (to ~)	приносить III / принести II (perf.)
brother	брат (m.)
build (to ~)	строить III / построить III (perf.)
building	здание (n.)
bun (bread roll)	булочка (f.)
burglary	взлом (m.)
burn (to ~)	гореть
bus	автобус (m.)
but	а, но
butter	масло (n.)
buy (to ~)	покупать / купить III (perf.)
bye!	пока!

C

camera	фотоаппарат (m.)
can	мочь / смочь (perf.)
Canada	Канада (f.)
Canadian (man)	канадец (m.)
Canadian (woman)	канадка (f.)
Canadian (adj.)	канадский
car (automobile)	автомашина, машина (f.)
car (of train)	вагон (m.)
carry (to ~)	носить III
cash	наличные (pl. only)
cash desk	касса (f.)
cash on delivery	наложенным платежом
castle	замок (m.)
celebrate (to ~)	праздновать
center	центр (m.)

change (to ~)	менять
change (to ~) (clothes)	переодеваться
chat (to ~)	разговаривать
cheap	дёшево
cheat (to ~)	обманывать
check (bill)	счёт (m.) (pl. счета)
check (cheque)	чек (m.)
check (to ~)	проверять
child	ребёнок (m.)
children	дети (irreg. pl.)
church	церковь (f.)
cigarette	сигарета (f.)
cigarette (short, unfiltered)	папироса (f.)
cinema (movie theater)	кино (=, n.), кинотеатр (m.)
citizen (man)	гражданин (m.)
citizen (woman)	гражданка (f.)
citizenship	гражданство (n.)
city	город (m.) (pl. города)
clever	умный
close (to ~)	закрывать / закрыть (perf.)
clothes	одежда (f. sg.)
cloud	облако (n.), (pl. облака)
coffee	кофе (m.)
cold	холодный
cold (sickness)	простуда (f.)
cold (to be ~)	мёрзнуть
cold (to have a ~)	простужен
color	цвет (m.) (pl. цвета)
come (to ~)	прийти II (perf.)
communicate (to ~)	сообщать / сообщить III (perf.)
compartment	купе (n.)
complain (to ~)	жаловаться
completely	совсем
complicated (hard)	сложный
concert	концерт (m.)
condom	презерватив (m.)
conductor	проводник (m.)
congratulate (to ~)	поздравлять
consulate	консульство (n.)
container	сосуд (m.)
contrary (on the ~!)	напротив!
conversation	разговор (m.)
cook (to ~) (to prepare a meal)	готовить
cook (to ~) (to heat food)	варить III
cooking	кухня (f.)
cool (temperature)	прохладный
correspond (to ~ with someone)	переписываться
corridor	коридор (m.)
costs (it ~)	(это) стоит
cosy	уютный
cotton wool	вата (f.)
count (to ~)	считать
country	страна (f.)
countryside	деревня (f.)
course (of ~)	конечно
crime	преступление (n.)
cry (to ~)	плакать
cure (to ~)	лечить III
currency	валюта (f.)
custom	обычай (m.)
customs	таможня (f.)

D

dance (to ~)	танцевать
dangerous	опасный
dark	тёмный
day	день (m.)
dead	мёртвый
death	смерть (f.)
decide (to ~)	решать
decoration	украшение (n.)
deep	глубокий
dentist	зубной врач (m.)
department store	универмаг (m.)

departure	выезд, отъезд (m.)	end	конец (m.)
detour	объезд, окольный путь (m.)	engine	мотор (m.)
		engine oil	моторное масло (n.)
diarrhea	понос (m.)	England	Англия (f.)
dictionary	словарь (m.)	English (in ~)	по-английски
die (to ~)	умирать	English (adj.)	английский
difficult	трудный	English (man)	англичанин (m.)
dinner	ужин (m.)	English (woman)	англичанка (f.)
dinner (to have ~)	ужинать / поужинать	enjoy oneself (to ~)	развлекаться
dirty	грязный	enough (that's ~!)	достаточно (adv.), довольно!
disco	дискотека (f.)		
do (to ~)	делать / сделать (perf.)	enter (to ~)	входить III
		enterprise	предприятие (n.)
doctor	врач (m.)	entrance	вход (m.)
document	документ (m.)	environment	окружение (n.)
documents	документы (m. pl.)	essential	обязательный
		euro	евро (=, m.)
dollar	доллар (m.)	evening	вечер (m.) (pl. вечера)
door	дверь (f.)		
dormitory	общежитие (n.)	every	каждый
drink	напиток (m.)	everyday (adj.)	ежедневный
drink (to ~)	пить II	every time	каждый раз
drop in on someone (to ~)	заходить III / зайти II (perf.)	everywhere	везде
		exact	точный
drunk	пьяный	exactly	точно
dry	сухой	excellent	отличный
during	во время	except	кроме
		exchange (to ~)	меняться
E		exchange (to ~) (things)	поменять (perf.)
earlier	раньше		
earlier than	прежде чем	exchange letters with someone (to ~) (to correspond)	переписываться
early	рано (adv.)		
earn (to ~)	зарабатывать		
earth	земля (f.)	excursion	экскурсия (f.)
east	восток (m.)	excuse me!	извините!
eat (to ~)	есть	exhibition	выставка (f.)
eat! (polite)	кушайте!	exit	выход (m.)
either... or...	или... или...	exit (to ~)	выходить III / выйти II (perf.)
embassy	посольство (n.)		
employee	служащий (m.)	expensive	дорогой
empty	пустой	explain (to ~)	объяснять

сто восемьдесят три **183**

export	вывоз *(m.)*, экспорт *(m.)*	flu	грипп *(m.)*
express (to ~)	выражать	fly (to ~)	летать *(unidir.)* / лететь III *(multidir.)*

F

fabric	ткань *(f.)*
fall (autumn)	осень *(f.)*
fall (to ~)	падать
famous	известный, знаменитый
far	далеко
fashion	мода *(f.)*
father	отец *(m.)*
fault	вина *(f.)*
fault (at ~)	виновный
fear (fright)	страх *(m.)*
fear (to ~)	бояться III
feel (to ~)	чувствовать
feeling	чувство *(n.)*
ferry	паром *(m.)*
fever	жар *(m.)*
few (not many)	мало...²
few (a ~)	несколько...²
field	поле *(n.)*
fill out (to ~) (a form)	заполнить
film	час *(m.)*
finally	наконец
find	находить III / найти II *(perf.)*
find out (to ~)	справляться
fine (penalty)	штраф *(m.)*
finger	палец *(m.)* *(pl.* пальцы*)*
finish (to ~)	оканчивать
fire	огонь *(m.)*
fish	рыба *(f.)*
flirt (to ~)	флиртировать
flirtation	флирт *(m.)*
flower	цветок *(m.)* *(pl.* цветы*)*
food	еда *(f.)*, кушанье *(f.)*, продовольствие *(n.)*
foot	нога *(f.)*
foot (on ~)	пешком
for (in exchange for / for a reason)	за...⁴
for (a purpose/ category)	для...²
for (a period of time)	на...⁴
forbidden	запрещён, запрещена *(f.)*, -но *(m.)*, -ны *(pl.)*
foreigner (man)	иностранец *(m.)*
foreigner (woman)	иностранка *(f.)*
forest	лес *(m.)* *(pl.* леса*)*
forget (to ~)	забывать / забыть *(perf.)*
fork	вилка *(f.)*
form	бланк *(m.)*
free	свободный
free of charge	бесплатный
fresh	свежий
friend (boyfriend)	друг *(m.)* *(pl.* друзья*)*
friend (girlfriend)	подруга *(f.)*
friendship	дружба *(f.)*
from (a place)	из...²
from (a person or a person's place)	от...²
fruit	фрукт *(m.)*
full	полный

G

garage (auto repairs)	автомастерская *(f.)*
gas	газ *(m.)*

gasoline (petrol)	бензин *(m.)*
get up (to ~)	вставать
girl (little girl)	девочка *(f.)*
girl (young woman)	девушка *(f.)*
give (to ~)	давать II / дать *(perf.)*
give back (to ~)	отдавать II / отдать *(perf.)*
glad	рад
glass (for drinking)	стакан *(m.)*
glass (material)	стекло *(n.)* (*pl.* стёкла)
glasses	очки *(pl.)*
go (to ~) (on foot)	идти II *(unidir.)* / ходить III *(multidir.)*
go (to ~) (by vehicle)	ехать *(unidir.)* / ездить III *(multidir.)*
God	бог *(m.)*
gold	золото *(n.)*
good	хороший *(adj.)*
good (well)	хорошо *(adv.)*
gram	грамм *(m.)*
greet (to ~)	приветствовать
greetings	привет *(m.)*
group	группа *(f.)*
guest	гость *(m.)*

H

half	половина *(f.)*
hand	рука *(f.)*
happiness	счастье *(n.)*
happy (fulfilled)	счастливый
happy (jolly, merry)	весёлый
harbor (port)	порт *(m.)*
hard (complicated)	сложный
hard (not soft)	твёрдый
hard-working	прилежный
have (to ~)	иметь
health	здоровье *(n.)*
healthy	здоровый
hear (to ~)	слышать / услышать III *(perf.)*
hi!	привет!
high	высокий
highway (motorway)	автомагистраль *(f.)*
history	история *(f.)*
hold in your hand (to ~)	держать в руке
hole	дыра *(f.)*
holiday (feast day)	праздник *(m.)*
home	дом *(m.)* (*pl.* дома)
hope (to ~)	надеяться
hospitality	гостеприимство *(n.)*
host	хозяин *(m.)*
hostel	общежитие *(n.)*
hostess	хозяйка *(f.)*
hotel	гостиница *(f.)*
hotel room	номер *(m.)* (*pl.* номера)
hour (time)	час *(m.)*
house	дом *(m.)* (*pl.* дома)
how	как
humid (damp)	сырой
hungry	голодный
hunt (to ~)	охотиться III
hurry (to ~)	торопиться III
hurts (it ~)	(это) болит *(3rd pers. sg.)*
husband	муж *(m.)* (*pl.* мужья)
husband and wife (married couple)	супруги *(pl.)*
hygiene	гигиена *(f.)*

I

ice	лёд *(m.)*
ice cream	мороженое *(n.)* (collective, no *pl.*)

if	если
if (interrogative particle)	ли
import	импорт (m.)
important	важный
in	в...⁴, в...⁶, на...⁴, на...⁶
industry	промышленность (f.)
inexpensive	недорого
inform (to ~)	сообщать / сообщить III (perf.); уведомлять
information	информация, справка (f.)
information desk	справочное бюро (n.)
injection	укол (m.)
injection (to give an ~)	делать укол
innocent	невинный
inside	внутри
instead of	вместо...²
insurance	страховка (f.)
interest (to ~)	интересовать
interest (to take an ~)	интересоваться
interesting	интересный
international	международный
into	в...⁴, на...⁴
invitation	приглашение (n.)
invite (to ~)	приглашать
Ireland	Ирландия (f.)
Irish (man)	ирландец (m.)
Irish (woman)	ирландка (f.)
Irish (adj.)	ирландский
iron (for clothes)	утюг (m.)
iron (to ~)	гладить III
island	остров (m.) (pl. острова)
it (e.g. it's hot)	это (n.)
item	штука (f.)

J

jeans	джинсы (pl. only)
journey	поездка (f.)

K

key	ключ (m.)
kill (to ~)	убивать
kiss	поцелуй (m.)
kiss (to ~)	целовать
kitchen	кухня (f.)
knife	нож (m.)
know (to ~)	знать

L

labor	труд (m.)
lake	озеро (n.) (pl. озёра)
lamp	лампа (f.)
land	земля (f.)
landscape	пейзаж (m.)
lane	переулок (m.)
language	язык (m.) (pl. языки)
late (it's ~)	поздно
late (to be ~)	опаздывать / опоздать (perf.)
laugh (to ~)	смеяться II
laundry (place)	прачечная (f.)
law	закон (m.)
lazy	ленивый
learn (to ~)	учиться III
leave (to ~) (by vehicle)	уезжать / уехать (unidir.)
leave (to ~) (by plane)	улетать / улететь III (perf.)
left	слева
left (on the ~)	налево
leg	нога (f.)
lend (to ~)	одалживать
letter (of alphabet)	буква (f.)
letter (missive)	письмо (n.)
lie down (to ~) III	лежать
life	жизнь (f.)

light (not heavy)	лёгкий	meet (to ~)	встречать
light (noun)	свет (m.)	meet (to ~) (each other)	встречаться
like (to ~) (lit. to please)	нравиться / понравиться	meet someone for the first time (to ~)	знакомиться III / познакомиться III (perf.)
like (to ~)	любить III	meeting	встреча (f.)
little (a ~)	немного	menu	меню (n.)
little (a ~) (of something)	немного...[2]	merchandise	товар (m.)
live (to ~)	жить II	mind (to keep in ~)	запоминать
located (is ~)	находится	minute	минута (f.)
located (to be ~)	находиться III	mistake	ошибка (f.)
long (for a long time)	долго (adv.)	mistake (to make a ~)	ошибаться
look (to ~)	смотреть	money	деньги (pl. only)
look for (to ~)	искать	month	месяц (m.)
lose (to ~)	терять / потерять (perf.)	more (than)	больше (чем)
lost (to get ~)	заблуждаться	morning	утро (n.)
loud	громкий	morning (in the ~)	утром
love	любовь (f.) (pl. любви)	mother	мать (f.) (pl. матери)
love (in ~)	влюблённый	motorboat	моторная лодка (f.)
love (to ~)	любить III	motorcycle	мотоцикл (m.)
lovely	прекрасный	motorway (highway)	автомагистраль (f.)
low	низкий	mountain	гора (f.)
luggage	багаж (m.)	move house (to ~)	переселяться
lunch	обед (m.)	movie theater (cinema)	кино (=, n.), кинотеатр (m.)
lunch (to have ~)	обедать	museum	музей (m.)
		music	музыка (f.)

M

make (to ~)	делать / сделать (perf.)		
make someone's acquaintance (to ~)	знакомиться III / познакомиться III (perf.)		

N

man	мужчина (m.)	naked	голый
many	много	name (first name)	имя (n.) (pl. имена)
map of Moscow	карта Москвы (f.)	napkin	салфетка (f.)
market	рынок (m.)	nationality (ethnic group)	национальность (f.)
match (to light)	спичка (f.)	nature	природа (f.)
material	материал (m.)	near (not for)	близко (adv.), недалеко
maybe	может быть		
meat	мясо (n.)		
medicine	лекарство (n.)		

necessary (it is ~)	надо *(impers.)*
need (to ~)	нужно *(impers.)*
needle	иголка *(f.)*
neither... nor	ни... ни
never	никогда
new	новый
New Zealand	Новая Зеландия *(f.)*
New Zealand (adj.)	новозеландский
New Zealander (man)	новозеландец *(m.)*
New Zealander (woman)	новозеландка *(f.)*
news	известие *(n. sg.)*
newspaper	газета *(f.)*
nice to meet you!	приятно!
night	ночь *(f.)*
no	нет
no one	никто
normal	нормальный
north	север *(m.)*
not	не
nothing	ничто
now	сейчас, теперь
number	номер *(m.) (pl.* номера*)*

O

occupation (profession)	профессия *(f.)*
occupied with (to be ~) (to do)	заниматься...[5]
offend (to ~)	обижать
office (bureau)	бюро *(=, n.)*
office worker	служащий *(m.)*
often	часто
oil	масло *(n.)*
old	старый
on (indicating a position or direction)	на...[4], на...[6]
on (a day of the week)	в...[4]
once	один раз
one	один / одна *(f.)*
only	только
onto	на...[4]
open (to ~)	открывать / открыть *(perf.)*
operator (telephone)	коммутатор *(m.)*
or	или
order	заказ *(m.)*
order (in ~ to)	чтобы
order (to ~)	заказывать / заказать *(perf.)*
organize (to ~)	организовать
other	другой
other (belonging to another)	чужой
outside (on the ~)	снаружи
owner	владелец *(m.)*
owner (home ~)	хозяин *(m.),* хозяйка *(f.)*

P

packet	пакет *(m.)*
pain	боль *(f.)*
pair (a ~)	папа *(m.)*
palace	дворец *(m.)*
paper	бумага *(f.)*
parcel (small ~)	бандероль *(f.)*
parents	родители *(pl. only)*
park	парк *(m.)*
park the car (to ~)	поставить машину III *(perf.)*
parking space	автостоянка *(f.)*
part (of)	часть (в)...[2]
passport	паспорт *(m.) (pl.* паспорта*)*
patient (medical)	пациент *(m.)*
pause	перерыв *(m.)*
pay (to ~)	платить III / заплатить III *(perf.)*
pencil	карандаш *(m.)*

people	люди *(pl. only)*, народ ("the people") *(m.)*	prepare (to ~)	готовить; приготавливать / приготовить III *(perf.)*
permission	разрешение *(n.)*		
permit (to ~)	разрешать		
person	человек *(m.)*, персона *(f.)*	present (to ~)	представлять / представить III *(perf.)*
perspire (to ~)	потеть	previously	раньше
petrol (gasoline)	бензин *(m.)*	price	цена *(f.)*
pharmacy	аптека *(f.)*	price for the journey	плата за проезд *(m.)*
photo	фото *(=, n.)*		
photograph (to ~)	фотографировать / сфотографировать *(perf.)*	private	частный
		problem	проблема *(f.)*
		program	программа *(f.)*
pick (someone) up (to ~)	заезжать за...[5]	pronunciation	произношение *(n.)*
		property	собственность *(f.)*
picture (painting – art –)	картина *(f.)*	propose (to ~)	предлагать
		pupil (boy)	ученик *(m.)*
pie	пирог *(m.)*	pupil (girl)	ученица *(f.)*
place	место *(n.)*	put (to ~) (something upright)	класть II / положить III *(perf.)*
plan	план *(m.)*		
plane	самолёт *(m.)*		
platform	платформа *(f.)*	put (to ~) (something flat)	ставить III / поставить III *(perf.)*
please	пожалуйста		
pleasure (with ~!)	охотно!		
poison	яд *(m.)*		
police	милиция *(f.)*		
policeman	милиционер *(m.)*	**Q**	
polite	вежливый	quality	качество *(n.)*
politics (policy)	политика *(f. sg.)*	quantity	количество *(n.)*
poor	бедный	quick!	быстро!
port (harbor)	порт *(m.)*	**R**	
position (geographical)	положение *(n.)*	radio	радио *(=, n.)*
possession (in one's ~)	у...[2]	railway station	вокзал *(m.)*
		rain	дождь *(m.)*
possible (it is ~) (allowed)	можно *(impers.)*	rare	редкий
		read (to ~)	читать / прочитать *(perf.)*
possible (it is ~)	возможно		
postcard	открытка *(f.)*		
post office	почта *(f.)*	ready!	готов!
poultry	птица *(f.)*	real (genuine)	действительный, настоящий
pound (sterling)	фунт *(m.)*		
pregnant	беременная		

сто восемьдесят девять **189**

receive (to ~)	получать / получить III (perf.)	run (to ~)	бежать III (unidir.) / бегать (multidir.)
recommend (to ~)	советовать	Russia	Россия (f.)
register (to ~) (a document)	прописывать, регистрировать	Russian (woman)	русская (f.)
		Russian (man)	русский (m.)
regular	регулярный	Russian (adj.)	русский
remember (to ~)	вспоминать	Russian (in ~)	по-русски
rent (for ~)	напрокат	Russian Federation	Российская Федерация (f.)
rent (to ~) (as the renter)	брать напрокат II		

S

rent out (to ~)	сдавать внаём
repair (renovation)	ремонт (m.)
repair (to ~) (to renovate)	ремонтировать
repeat (to ~)	повторять / повторить III (perf.)
request	просьба (f.)
reservation (train)	плацкарта (f.)
reserve (to ~) (to book)	бронировать / забронировать (perf.)
resident	житель (m.)
responsibility	ответственность (f.)
rest (to ~) (to relax)	отдыхать
rich	богатый
right	справа
right (correct)	правильный
right (legal right)	право (n.)
right (on the ~)	направо
river	река (f.)
road	дорога (f.)
road map	дорожная карта (f.)
room	комната (f.)
rope	трос (m.)
rotten	гнилой
ruble	рубль (m.)
rude (crude)	грубый

sad	печальный
sanitary napkin	подкладка (f.)
save money (to ~)	экономить III
say (to ~)	говорить III / сказать (perf.)
say goodbye (to ~)	прощаться
scenery	пейзаж (m.)
school	школа (f.)
scissors	ножницы (pl. only)
Scot (man)	шотландец (m.)
Scot (woman)	шотландка (f.)
Scotland	Шотландия (f.)
Scottish (adj.)	шотландский
sea	море (n.)
season	время года (n.)
seat (on transport, in a theatre)	место (n.)
seated (to be ~)	сидеть III
second (noun)	секунда (f.)
see (to ~)	видеть III
see each other (to ~)	видеться III
sell (to ~)	продавать II
send (to ~)	посылать
service	обслуживание (n.)
service station	бензопункт (m.)
set	комплект (m.)
sharp	острый
sheets	бельё (n.)
ship	судно (n.) (pl. судна)

shoes	обувь (f. sg.)	speak (to ~)	говорить III / сказать (perf.)
shoot (to ~)	стрелять		
shop	магазин (m.)	spend the night (to ~)	ночевать / переночевать (perf.)
short	короткий		
show (to ~)	показывать / показать (perf.)		
		spicy	острый
sick	больной, болен	spoon	ложка (f.)
sickness	болезнь (f.)	sport	спорт (m.)
sign (to ~)	подписывать / подписать (perf.)	spring	весна (f.)
		square (in city)	площадь (f.)
silver	серебро (n.)	staircase	лестница (f.)
simple	простой	stamp (postage ~)	(почтовая) марка (f.)
simply	просто		
since then	с тех пор	stand (to ~)	стоять III
sing (to ~)	петь	start	начало (n.)
sister	сестра (f.) (pl. сёстры)	start (to ~)	начинать / начать II (perf.)
sit down (to ~)	садиться III / сесть (perf.)	station (transport)	остановка (f.)
		stay	пребывание (n.)
sky	небо (n.)	stay (to ~)	оставаться II / остаться (perf.)
sleep (to ~)	спать III		
slow	медленный		
small	маленький	still	ещё
small change	мелочь (f.)	stone	камень (m.)
smile (to ~)	улыбаться	stop (station)	остановка (f.)
smoke (to ~)	курить III	stop (to ~) (someone or something)	останавливать / остановить III (perf.)
snow	снег (m.) (pl. снега)		
so	так	stop (to ~) (doing something)	переставать II
soap	мыло (n.)		
society	общество (n.)	storm	гроза (f.)
some	несколько	story	рассказ (m.)
someone	кто-нибудь	strange	любопытно
sometimes	иногда	street	улица (f.)
son	сын (m.) (pl. сыновья)	stroll	прогулка (f.)
		stroll (to ~)	прогуливаться
song	песня (f.)	strong (person, will, smell, etc.)	сильный
soon	скоро		
sorry!	извините!	strong (person, wine, etc.)	крепкий
soup	суп (m.)		
south	юг (m.)	student (male)	студент (m.)
spare part	запасная часть (f.)	student (female)	студентка (f.)
		stupid	глупый
		success	успех (m.)
		sudden(ly)	вдруг

suits (it ~) (clothes)	сидит
summer	лето (n.)
sun	солнце (n.)
surname	фамилия (f.)
sweet	сладкий
swim (to ~)	плавать
swim (to ~) (to go bathing)	купаться
swindle (to ~)	обманывать
syringe	шприц (m.)

T

tablet (pill)	таблетка (f.)
take (to ~) (umbrella, taxi, etc.)	брать II / взять II (perf.)
take (to ~) (a shower, medicine, a decision, etc.)	принимать
take a shower (to ~)	принимать душ
talk (to ~)	разговаривать
tall	высокий
taste (to ~)	пробовать
tasty (delicious)	вкусный
tax (duty)	пошлина (f.)
taxi	такси (=, n.)
tea	чай (m.)
teach (to ~)	обучать
telegram	телеграмма (f.)
telephone	телефон (m.)
telephone (to ~)	звонить III / позвонить III (по телефону)
television	телевизор (m.)
tell (to ~) (a story)	рассказывать / рассказать (perf.)
tent	палатка (f.)
territory	территория (f.)
than	чем
thank you	спасибо
thanks to	благодаря...[3]
that (pronoun) (e.g. that's him!)	это (n.)
that (demonstrative article) (e.g. that boy)	этот/эта/это (m./f./n.)
that one	тот (m.)
theater	театр (m.)
theft (robbery)	кража (f.)
there (to ~)	туда
there is	есть (impers.)
there is no	нет...[2]
therefore	так
thin	тонкий
think (to ~)	думать
those	те (pl.)
through	через...[4]
ticket	билет (m.)
ticket booth	касса (f.)
tight	тесный
time	время (n.) час (m.)
time (in ~)	вовремя
timetable	расписание (n.)
tip (money)	чаевые (pl. only)
tire (of car)	шина (f.)
tired	усталый
to (direction)	в...[4], на...[4]
to (someone's house)	к...[3]
tobacco	табак (m.)
together	вместе
toilet	туалет (m.)
toilet paper	туалетная бумага (f.)
tomorrow	завтра
too many	слишком (много)
toothpaste	зубная паста (f.)
top (on the ~)	наверху
total	сумма (f.)
tour (a ~)	экскурсия (f.)
tourist (man)	турист (m.)
tourist (woman)	туристка (f.)

tourist sight	достопримечательность (f.)
tow a car (to ~)	взять II (perf.) машину на буксир
towel	полотенце (n.)
tower	башня (f.)
toy	игрушка (f.)
trade	торговля (f.)
tradition	традиция (f.)
train	поезд (m.) (pl. поезда)
tram	трамвай (m.)
translate (to ~)	переводить III / перевести II (perf.)
translator (man)	переводчик (m.)
translator (woman)	переводчица (f.)
travel (to ~)	путешествовать
travel agency	бюро путешествий (n.)
truth	правда (f.)
try (to ~)	пробовать
turn (to ~)	сворачивать / свернуть II (perf.)

U

under	под...⁴...⁵
underneath	внизу
understand (to ~)	понимать / понять II (perf.)
undress (to ~)	раздевать
university	университет (m.)
unknown	незнакомый
unnecessary	ненужный
until	до...²
up	наверх
urgent	срочный
urgently	срочно (adv.)
use (to ~)	пользоваться
usually	обычно

V

vacant	свободный
vacation	каникулы (pl. only)
vacation (leave from work)	отпуск (m.) (pl. отпуска)
vaccinate (to ~)	прививать
vaccination	прививка (f.)
valley	долина (f.)
vegetables	овощи (m. pl.)
venomous snake	ядовитая змея (f.)
very	очень
village	деревня (f.)
visit (official)	визит (m.)
visit	посещение (n.)
visit (to ~) (a place)	осматривать / осмотреть III (perf.)
visit (to ~) (a place)	посещать / посетить III (perf.)
voice	голос (m.) (pl. голоса)

W

wait for (to ~)	ждать II, подождать II
waiter	официант (m.)
waitress	официантка (f.)
wall	стена (f.)
wake (someone)	будить III / разбудить III (perf.)
wander (to ~)	бродить III
want (to ~)	хотеть
warm	тёплый
wash (to ~)	мыть
watch (timepiece)	часы (pl. only)
watch (to ~)	смотреть III
water	вода (f.)
weather	погода (f.)
wedding	свадьба (f.)
week	неделя (f.)

сто девяносто три

weight	**вес** *(m.)*
welcoming	**приветливый**
well	**хорошо** *(adv.)*
west	**запад** *(m.)*
wet	**мокрый**
wheel	**колесо** *(n.)* (*pl.* **колёса**)
when	**когда**
where	**где**
where (to ~)	**куда**
wide	**широкий**
wife	**жена** *(f.)* (*pl.* **жёны**)
win (to ~)	**выигрывать**
wind	**ветер** *(m.)*
window	**окно** *(n.)*
winter	**зима** *(f.)*
wish (to ~)	**желать**
with	**с...**[5]
without	**без...**[2]
woman	**женщина** *(f.)*
wood	**дерево** *(n.)*
word	**слово** *(n.)*
work (labor)	**труд** *(m.)*
work	**работа** *(f.)*
work (to ~)	**работать**
working (is not ~)	**не работает**
workshop	**мастерская** *(f.)*
wound (injury)	**рана** *(f.)*
write (to ~)	**писать / написать**
wrong (that's ~!)	**неправильно!**
wrong (in the ~)	**виновный**

Y

year	**год** *(m.)*
yell (to ~)	**кричать** III
yes	**да**
yesterday	**вчера**
young	**молодой**
younger than	**моложе чем**

Z

zoo	**зоопарк** *(m.)*

Achevé d'imprimer par Corlet, Imprimeur, S.A. - 14110 Condé-sur-Noireau
N° d'édition : 2967 - N° d'Imprimeur : 135291 - Dépôt légal : janvier 2011
Imprimé en France